GW00499282

SUNLIGHT

First published in 2018 by
The Dedalus Press
13 Moyclare Road
Baldoyle
Dublin D13 K1C2
Ireland

www.**dedaluspress**.com

ISBN 978 1 910251 31 7

Dedalus Press titles are represented in the UK by
Inpress Books, www.inpressbooks.co.uk,
and in North America by Syracuse University Press, Inc.,
www.syracuseuniversitypress.syr.edu.

Cover image: 'Rooms by the Sea' (detail) by Edward Hopper
1951, oil on canvas, 74.3 x 101.6 cm (29 1/4 x 40 in.)
Yale University Art Gallery
Bequest of Stephen Carlton Clark, B.A. 1903

The Dedalus Press receives financial assistance from
The Arts Council / An Chomhairle Ealaíon.

SUNLIGHT
New and Selected Poems

JOHN O'DONNELL

DEDALUS PRESS

ACKNOWLEDGEMENTS

Grateful acknowledgements are due to the editors of all publications in which the earlier poems, or version of them, appeared, as well as to the editors of the following in which a number of the new poems were first published: *The Irish Times, Irish Poetry Reading Archive* (UCD Library), *Metamorphic: 21ˢᵗ Century Poets respond to Ovid*, eds. Nessa O'Mahony and Paul Munden (Recent Work Press, 2017), *Poetry Ireland Review, Reading The Future*, ed. Alan Hayes (Arlen House, 2018), *The Recorder* (USA), *Sunday Miscellany* (RTÉ Radio 1) and *Words by Water*.

'Some Other Country' won the Hennessy New Irish Writing Award for Poetry; 'Kola's Shop' won the Ireland Funds Prize; 'The Majestic' won the SeaCat Irish National Poetry Competition; 'Chinese Lantern' won the Irish Times/Anna Livia Poetry Award; 'Icarus Sees His Father Fly' won the Listowel Writers Week Poetry Prize.

Thanks also to Michael Bevan, Sue Booth-Forbes (Anam Cara), Ursula Byrne, Ciaran Carty, Brendan Flynn, Seamus Hosey, Maureen Kennelly and all at Poetry Ireland, Maire Logue, Eilish Wren and all at Listowel Writers' Week, Joan McBreen, the late Tom O'Dea, Gerard Smyth, all at 100 St. Stephens Green, the late Caroline Walsh, and Yve Williams.

Special thanks to Niall MacMonagle for his kind introduction to this collection. And to my father, my sister Catherine and my brothers Nick and Michael, and – especially – to Michelene, William, Jack, Eavan and Tom, with love.

CONTENTS

*

⏝

from **On Water** (2014)

⤚

New Poems

⤚

To the memory of Mary O'Donnell 1933–2015

sunlight on the ocean, shining still

Introduction

"As long as you read this poem
I will be writing it. "
—Alden Nowlan, 'An Exchange of Gifts'

E VERY POEM IS PRESENT. In its making, the poem is intensely present to the poet, and that it is present too, for the reader, when that same poem is being read, days, years or centuries later, is poetry's strange, remarkable and special power. Reading poetry is an intimate experience. The rest of the world falls away; a voice on the page becomes the voice inside your head and in this one-to-one exchange the poem's inner life, its thoughts, its feelings, its ideas, its music live again. What Aidan Mathews calls "the intimacy of print" creates, in Mathews's words, "a community of very different dead and dying readers", and this sober observation reminds us that each reading becomes at once, paradoxically, not only a separate and shared experience but an on-going one.

Time not only surrounds and inhabits the writing and reading of poetry but it is one of poetry's vital and recurring themes. Love, loss, memory, history, place are other familiar preoccupations in John O'Donnell's work and, though poetry's subject matter may be similar, a unique voice will explore these themes in unique ways.

Poetry's first impulse is lyrical. John O'Donnell's poetry is lyrical and his poetry also combines narrative and dramatic qualities in both his private and public poems. Lyric, narrative and dramatic qualities are found in 'Volpi', the poem that opens this book, *Sunlight*, O'Donnell's *New and Selected*. It seems right that in this poem O'Donnell brings his reader back to a time and place when his imagination was stirred by an eccentric teacher. With admirable, unsettling honesty, O'Donnell paints a vivid portrait of insensitive, cruel adolescents but also reminds us of the 'glamour' and the 'danger' of invention and creativity. Here, O'Donnell is on high alert and, again and again, the occasions that have prompted the poems in this collection begin with a disciplined observation that leads to insight, understanding. And, as with all poetry, how something is said is more important than what is being said.

Attentive to different speech acts, O'Donnell, a versatile poet, writes sonnet sequences, poems in couplets, tercets, quatrains, a list poem, prose poems. In 'Where A Poem Comes From' from O'Donnell's second collection *Icarus Sees His Father Fly* [2004] he speaks of this wonderful and mysterious thing – the making of a poem – using a simple, memorable image. A ten-year-old O'Donnell falls off a roof at the back of an abandoned house, a house he says "I'd long been warned against". Losing his footing due to carelessness, day-dreaming or perhaps pure chance, we are offered a valuable glimpse into the making of poetry. You've got to be adventurous, he suggests, take risks, and then the carelessness, the day-dreaming, the chance element all combine to create the well-made poem on the page. A fall, a rusted spike, a throbbing, a scar not only add a realistic touch but such details let us know that flights of fancy have their price.

On winning the SeaCat Irish National Poetry Competition in 2002, O'Donnell said "I write poetry on all aspects of life" and O'Donnell's work ranges wide. The poems collected here take us very different places, sometimes back in time to the monks on Skellig, Hugh O'Neill's Rome, James Joyce opening Ireland's first cinema in 1909, the Holocaust, pioneering in Oregon, Shakespeare in Ireland, a grandmother's Alzheimer's. Poems explore topics as varied as sports day, rhino hunting, emigration, a father-son relationship, sailing, being taught golf; there's also a tender love poem to his daughter. O'Donnell remembers well what being young is like: In that SeaCat prize-winning poem 'The Majestic', the excitement, the uncertainties of teenagers in a darkened cinema on first dates on rain-filled summer afternoons, are convincingly captured in an image of boys in "row on row/ of one-armed crucifixions waiting for the action/ to begin ... We were young and scared/ of nothing except heartbreak."

Here is a poet who searches for truth and, whether O'Donnell is remembering "me, surly in a sleeping-bag, fifteen" or the ugliness of racism and xenophobia, the Omagh atrocity or his visit to an optician, the voice is always direct and honest. In a nine-line poem, 'What The Tide Brings In,' the reader is lulled in with easy, colourful, deliberately lyrical images – until the final line, remembering Ireland's dark past, packs its punch.

What The Tide Brings In

A wounded star. Crabs in battle-dress.
Salt chorus of a thousand shells. Slumped
blancmange of jellyfish on ochre beach.
A slatted crate that once held oranges. A ball
kicked brightly out of reach. Whale songs.
Kitchen suds. Bladderwrack laid out
in Sunday duds. A ribboned hat,
sunny gust from First Class Deck.
An unnamed bundle in a fertiliser sack.

The three sonnet sequences, New Testimonies, This Child and On Water, give voice to those who witnessed momentous Biblical events and reveal an empathetic curiosity. Cliché is the enemy of poetry and in these Biblical scenarios when a servant, a soldier, Barabbas, Pilate, an innkeeper's daughter, Joseph, the camel boy, a wedding guest report the extraordinary in calm, detached, colloquial tones, O'Donnell makes it new.

The poems in *New and Selected* are carefully arranged and highlight O'Donnell's keen awareness of different aspects of a similar topic. In 'Some Other Country', another one of

O'Donnell's many prize-winning poems, he asks what those who were forced to emigrate would make of boomtime Ireland. This poem looks at the emigrant Irish, "Wide-eyed, gazing upwards/ At high glass and shining steel"; it is followed by the powerful, disturbing 'Kola's Shop'. Emigrant and immigrant side by side. A passionate awareness of social issues informs the poem in which the hard-working Kola is accused and abused: "The night before/ a letter shoved in underneath the door/warned Kola, 'keep your monkey kids/ away from ours, we don't want your AIDS'". A similar and effective contrast is found when the lonely, tender love poem 'Watching Stars' precedes 'The Shipping Forecast', the first a father-son poem from a father's perspective, the second from a teenage son's point of view. And later, among the New Poems, when we come across 'Nighthawks', a poem this time addressed to his mother, we come across a poem that is sad and courageous and clear-sighted. Such poems speak to each other and in doing so weave an engaging narrative.

In poems that remember Michael Hartnett, Caroline Walsh, Seamus Heaney, family, friends, in poems that celebrate Tony O'Malley and John Shinnors, the voice is affectionate and serious. But O'Donnell is also capable of a light, playful touch as in 'Roll Call' where, in an A-Z sequence, he remembers and invents a colourful gallery of classmates, some of whom are rogues, others are idiosyncratic, rebellious individuals and in a wacky 'Rowing to America', the speaker finds a flying fish "flipflipping/ iridescence at my feet" and devours it whole.

In John O'Donnell's work, image and rhythm, essential to poetry, are seen and heard.

Denis Donoghue believes metaphors 'give us more abundant life … they add perceptions that were not there before' and O'Donnell makes striking and memorable connections. In 'Mackerel', the speaker is carrying a coffin, carrying "the weight of what's in there with you, bowlines/ and anchor-chain and South Sea frangipani". Here and elsewhere, vivid pictures abound: the threatened rhino is a "god// in robes of crumpled iron"; a terrified de Valera is "buttoned up for his first flight"; in 'Sunlight' he sees "the sun's early brilliance landing/ on the bedclothes, on the tubes and dials and switches,/ and on the slumped flesh, the sunken cheekbones of my mother" and confesses with remarkable honesty that the moment prompted "this shameless// brutal impulse to make art".

Or the haiku which manages, in just seventeen syllables, a narrative that captures a happy wedding, past tense, and a present-tense, fractured family:

> Cherry blossoms strewn
> outside the women's shelter.
> Last year's confetti.

Or how in 'Café':

> Night presses its nose against the glass,
> but this brightness within declares
> a larger lonely

In longer, sustained narrative poems, such as 'Kecksies', 'Portrait of a Young Woman', 'Nighthawks', 'The Breaststroke', where what is not said or unsaid is as important as what is said, O'Donnell proves he is up to the challenge and captures the close-up and personal with a wonderful fluency. Without rhythm there is no poetry. We hear in O'Donnell's deftly handled rhyme, slant-rhyme, the run-on line its distinctive music.

Every poem, of course, is also about poetry. 'Postcard' obviously is. Tracing, as it does, a movement from inspiration to achievement, the sonnet concludes that though "the words for all this" can be found, O'Donnell acknowledges that there's "no knowing where the next is coming from". In 'The Lucas Planet

No. 33', O'Donnell's fitting tribute to Seamus Heaney, he is "uncertain where I'm going". But a chrome plated bicycle kerosene lamp from the 1930s illuminates a road that becomes a funeral journey, that becomes a legacy. In that same poem O'Donnell acknowledges how Heaney inspires him to keep going. What all poets believe, "the credo of all art: to make the effort made seem effortless while going/ to the heart of what matters", is true for John O'Donnell; it is O'Donnell's belief and it is his achievement.

We go to poetry for many reasons. "We go to poetry," says Adrienne Rich, "because we believe it has something to do with us. We also go to poetry to receive the experience of the *not me*, enter a field of vision we could not otherwise comprehend." In this book the reader is invited to do both and there is a sense that John O'Donnell has somehow heeded Jack Kerouac's advice to writers: "be in love with your life" and "accept loss forever".

A *New and Selected*, as the title suggests, does two things: it's a mini-retrospective but it also lets us know what Plath knew: that "the blood-jet is poetry; there is no stopping it." There's a generous selection from O'Donnell's three volumes, *Some Other Country*, *Icarus Sees His Father Fly* and *On Water*, and the new poems included here prove that O'Donnell is certainly keeping going. His poems have been widely published and broadcast in Ireland and abroad. His poem 'Beads', written at a time when the Ryan Commission was reporting, was broadcast on RTÉ's *Morning Ireland;* it is powerful and honest in its controlled and contained, understated condemnation of gross injustice, as well as proof that a poem truly is the news that stays news.

O'Donnell's poetry explores the steady and steadying presence of love within a family context but it also gives us the bigger picture, pictures of injustice, turmoil, 'the unfathomable' and what O'Donnell calls "a deep darker than ink". When Sara Berkeley says "Alone I turn to poetry and poetry turns to me" she is recognising its true worth, its ability to speak directly to us, that precious and intimate relationship between poet and reader. Turn to these enriching and engaging poems in *Sunlight: New and Selected Poems*; the poems will turn to you. And you will be rewarded.

— Niall MacMonagle

from **Some Other Country (2002)**

Volpi

He should have been an Italian tenor, belting out the high ones
in Carnegie and adoring the applause, the rattle of their jewellery
instead of pencil-cases, rulers as we fidgeted in class, half-listening
while he interrupted the conjugation of a difficult French verb
and swished his gown back like a curtain to show us all
another excerpt from the movie of his life. Such glamour
and such danger: how he'd stood out on the wing of a plane
at thirty thousand feet, or climbed into the mouth of a volcano
so as to pluck a fallen infant from the boiling lava. And never
Sir or Mister; always, always *Signor* Volpi, which he explained
was close to vulpine, fox-like (though he was naturally a direct
descendant of the wolf-cub who built Rome). His once-great brush
long gone; just a couple of grey strands held in place with hair-oil.
Smirking we laid traps for him, alarm clocks going off in cupboards,
the duster studded with match-heads lighting like a flare in his hand
as he tried to wipe the blackboard clean. The more we disbelieved
the more the stories grew: we shivered in our singlets at Gymnastics,
sniggering as he taught us how to march like Mussolini. Slowly we
closed in, his face purpling with shock when the banger went off at
        the back;
outright laughter as he recalled his role in the Charge of the Light
        Brigade,
and not forgetting of course the time his back was turned when we
heaved every desk right up to where he stood, surrounding him.
        And his
high-pitched scream. And how, when he came back to say goodbye
three months later, having been 'out sick' he hobbled on a little cane,
one foot dragging loose where the teeth of the snare had been.

Wren Night

in memoriam Michael Hartnett

Wind is building out at sea
as the music keeps on coming,
one tune following the other
like seagulls in bad weather,
swooping low then rising up

inside the little room. The money
they'd collected spent, the snug
is dizzy with Christmas decorations:
ashtrays, beermats, bodhrans,
and pints of porter roosting

underneath the windowed moon.
Now a small man in a cap
is standing up to sing
an air as old as birdsong,
cigarette and drink forgotten;

his turn cannot come too soon.
The listeners leafy-still. Eyes closed,
head back, he throws his pink beak
open, gives out each note as if
his life depended on the tune.

What The Tide Brings In

A wounded star. Crabs in battledress.
Salt chorus of a thousand shells. Slumped
blancmange of jellyfish on ochre beach.
A slatted crate that once held oranges. A ball
kicked brightly out of reach. Whale songs.
Kitchen suds. Bladderwrack laid out
in Sunday duds. A ribboned hat,
sunny gust from First Class Deck.
An unnamed bundle in a fertiliser sack.

Sports Day

Suburban pastoral, this: off-white sky,
desultory screech of tannoy; medalled
winners in a swoon of bliss. Her new
partner in tow, the red-nailed mother glides
past paunchy dads consoling flat-foot sons

who'll later cheer them in the Father's Race
as they lollop puff-cheeked towards the line,
the near-seizure worth it to save face. End of term;
loss thickens in the air, in stifled classrooms,
empty: *what now* whisper the corridors, the stairs,

What now? The egg-and-spoon
of marriage? The workplace tug-of-war?
Outside at the finish, *sturm und drang*;
the hundred metres is close-run. For every boy
breasting the tape there are, will be

so many also-rans, who'll prise open
the future's oyster-shell to find a world
of sand instead of pearl. How they
clamour as they line up, eager at the start,
flush-faced and staring down the track

as if it were the barrel of a gun,
listening for the starting-pistol's crack
that sends them scampering away
from all of this, bright rags of colour
streaming out into a dying sun.

Rhino

Commotion at the water-hole as he approaches,
a shuffling of armour scattering the dust.
Nervy gazelles skitter at the edge as
he stomps into the shallows, past

flusters of flamingos, the little tick bird
lording it on his back. A square-lipped
scowl lowered; from the still water is heard
a guzzling and a greedy gulping, lusty god

in robes of crumpled iron. Above him
parakeets jeer but keep their distance,
this muddy basin his brute kingdom
till he's sated. Bush-shadows, inference

of voices; the great head lifts and turns,
scenting the air. Once these porthole eyes
watched dinosaurs like super-tankers roam the plains.
But now he blinks, straining in the haze

to shape the blurs that stare back
from leaf-light as he sniffs once more, inhaling
the sweat-soaked shirts, the oily reek
of gunmetal. Warning screeches in the wing-

flapped air, but there's no holding him,
the terrible head-spikes angled for the charge.
Thunder underfoot, but all he hears is the blood-drum
bang in brain as he rumbles in grey rage

into the barrel-flash, smoke rising from the muzzle,
then staggers in a slow-motion capsize.

One last bewildered moan. Becomes history, huge fossil
as the men advance, wary at first, then later cries

of triumph. The dull clack of machete blade;
overhead the vultures fly a holding pattern.
On the ground the horns wait to be mounted,
each one a sad lopped-off erection.

New Testimonies

Then the high priest rent his clothes and saith,
What need we any further witness?
Ye have heard the blasphemy: what think ye?
—Mark 14:63, 64

I. The Landlord's Basin

The booking was for thirteen; we put them
In the function room upstairs. More trouble
Than they're worth, these meals at Passover,
And we were busy, so I don't remember
Much about the night, you understand. They'd
The usual: lamb, of course, and matzo-bread
And wine. One of them came down, asked
For a towel. So nervy he was; twitchy, pale.
He trudged back up but later on I saw him
Slipping out the side, before the rest.
Afterwards I went in to clear up. I can't say
I saw any sign of something ended or begun:
Just a basin, full of dirty water; and the mice, already
Moving in among the bones and crumbs.

II. A Captain's Report

Sir: I am to report to you as follows:
In accordance with your order the arrest
Was made at 0200 hours last night
In a nearby public park. By then quite
A crowd had gathered, and there were at first
Some scuffles when our contact gave the sign
(Ingenious, if I may say, the kiss).
He did not struggle and appeared resigned
When we took him: we were, of course, well-armed.
The three with him were bleary-eyed and scared;
One lashed out at a servant standing near.
I feared the worst, prepared to draw my sword
Until the prisoner touched the bloodied ear
Which later healed, it seems; this was unconfirmed.

III. Barabbas

I'd heard the voices outside in the square;
So strange to hear them shouting out my name.
Suddenly, the guard's opening the cell;
I didn't hang about then, I can tell you:
I just scarpered, wondering where I'd find
Enough money for a whore, and some wine.
I tried to blag a little stall, but the owner
Chased me off; it didn't seem the same
Somehow. Perhaps I'd lost my nerve.
Soon afterwards The Movement were on,
Telling me that I'd become a hero now.
But I left town. And kept thinking of how
I'd glanced back once, but he was already gone.
And whether we'd both got what we deserve.

IV. The Cross Speaks

Years before, I sprouted from the ground,
Spindly, awkward, reaching for the light.
Rains came. I grew taller, watched the land
Unfolding below me. My limbs stretched out
To feel bird-scratch, buds straining into leaf.
I sucked up earthy juices, dug in deep
Until hewn, rough-cut to upright and crossbeam.
The driven nails splitting the grain; nape of neck.
Then hoisted up. On either side the screams
Of dying men. Thunder in the bruise-dark sky;
Beneath me soldiers, clack of dice. One last cry
Then he was gone, the slung rib cage hung slack.
Splintered into kindling, I took flame; became
Smoke billowing from ash. And rose again.

V. Pilate Explains

Easy for you all today to blame
My failure then to take a firmer line.
The baying crowd that day was just the same;
Yellow-eyed, and stinking of cheap wine,
So quick to point the finger. And as if
All that wasn't enough, there's the wife
Who hated living here from the start
Elbowing my ribs about some dream she'd
Had where *he* appeared; well, have a heart:
What would you have done? I'll certainly plead
Guilty as the next man to being weak, but
Think while you prepare the noose of history
In the end it turned out what I did was right:
Where would you be now if I had set him free?

VI. Kitchen Girl at Emmaus

It was late, and I'd already plenty
To be doing, dishes to wash and dry,
The floor to sweep, but the master was insistent we
Stayed open when the three of them arrived.
I could hear their voices through the hatch,
Two of them talking nineteen to the dozen
About the rumours earlier that day which
I would not believe, it still doesn't
Make sense, a dead body going missing
Just like that. The third one had his back to me;
I couldn't quite make out the things he said.
The others seemed to find his words confusing;
The room silent when I brought the food, till he
Reached out – those hands! - to take the bread.

O'Neill in Rome

Here the ruthless opulence unnerves me.
I miss thatch-smoke and the stench of cattle
In night-time raids as taut as a bow bending,
The ditch and thorn in league with us as we
Stole what was ours. Amongst whispers and the rattle
Of informers' coins my vision blurs, is ending

In shadows of a weakened evening sun
Watched over tidied fields. And broken hills
Mountjoy still swaggers on; red wine spills from my hand
As I awake from dreams of battles won
To the absence history's glinting blade fulfils:
Beneath the smashed stone seat the furtive plots of land.

Plush, Oregon

Days lean against each other in Newmarket
like shovels stacked in Hardware at the store
where he bustles between shelves and counters,
eager in a clean apprentice apron.
A shadow in the doorway, stetson
high as a white stallion's head,
wants gloves, the toughest, forty pairs,
for land in Oregon, where you can own
as much as you can fence. The boy's fingers
fumble to untie the apron-strings;
down the narrowed streets he hurries after
towards the quays, lurch of ocean.
Salt prayers on his lips at Immigration,
the bag his father gave held tighter still.

In the blue dawn he awakens under canvas,
stares out over unbroken mountains; there's more here
than his mind can ever fill. The sun
splinters his head: a dead horse is alive
with flies. He tries to nail down the landscape,
feels pain blistering within, a place he cannot name.
Indians are watchful, sullen, but will trade
buffalo hides and stones for grinding corn on
(worn flat, miles from any wave-washed shore),
for whiskey and spent cartridges.
At night the ranchers teach them to play poker,
stashed aces and sly glances in the firelight.
One Indian holds out proud a hand of diamonds
then, smiling, stumbles on the white man's word: 'Plush'.
He fingers the cards, needing hearts,
thinks of the girls giggling in Haberdashery.
In his pocket the smooth stone dreams of the sea.

Idle Corner

At the Famine Exhibition
we swallow history. That men
each ate a stone of potatoes daily,
we are told, and shown
a plate heaped high with tubers,
sprout-eyed, useless. Here is a room
where ten or twelve might live,
and over there a map displays
the spray of voyages of ships
leaving, leaving. There is

more: food-queues,
the slammed doors of workhouses
and people laying down walls and roads
that went nowhere. This is such a road,
begun near a crossroads that was known

as 'Idle Corner'. Here men and women
waited to be called to build,
summoned to replace a friend
who'd fallen, his body carried back
past where they stood. And no one spoke.
Days and nights they waited
for a voice to come, until
in the end none came, and the road

died out amid scutch grass
and silence heard here still. The words
for all of this are gone, buried
under stones or in wet ditches,
or slid over the side
of a small ship straining in the Atlantic.

Anchor

The village basks in the afternoon. Locals stroll the streets
like movie-stars, or loll in cars that slumber round the square.
Through a passenger window I watch fishermen
fat as salmon inspect *The Cork Examiner*, declining
'Problems of Anorexic Males' for a forecast
of tomorrow's match. Eased over the bar
my uncle is explaining how once, in America, he'd singlehanded
    had to
stop a train — in an emergency. His moored companions
drink in holy silence.

He sighs. Beyond the playground ocean subway cars
are trawling through New York and Boston, hauling
boys from Gougane Barra and Coomhola towards offices and
    jobs.
Tonight, fearing I am once again at sea, I find I am
held fast by that stilled moment, an anchor
bedded in the harbour sand. Beside the chain-links
startled shoals rush by.

Some Other Country

On humming streets the gleaming cars parade,
Announcing boom; the whole place
In the money, making music.
Chorus-lines of cranes swing
In time to the new tune wafting out
From restaurants and café-bars, loud refrain

Of bronzed accents singing songs of gold.
Houses and hotels are blooming everywhere,
Apartment-blocks sprouting overnight
Like fairy-rings in silent fields and
Quaysides from where others sailed before
On crowded narrow ships,
Clutching their bundled miseries.

What would they have made of all of this?
They did not choose to leave, and yet
When they went they left behind
Far more than cousins or exhausted farms:
They sent money back in parcels, but they left us
Possibilities; the chance to decide
What it was we wanted, and
The opportunity to shape it

Into what they also must have seen,
Huddled on the gangplank in the harbour,
Wide-eyed, gazing upwards
At high glass and shining steel
And hearing amid the clamour and
The welcomes loaded with ambiguities
Other voices struggling to find

A language adequate to exile
In some other country
They would never quite recognise
As their own.

Kola's Shop

Kola's shop sells fufu flour and okra,
brown beans, egg plant and cassava,
goat's meat and bitter-leaf. He's open early,
earlier than the other stores nearby,

unlocking the till, checking stocks of crayfish
and couscous as the city yawns and stretches,
scratching itself. In the back you can play pool,
use the International phone to make a call,

you can even get your hair cut
too, though mostly it's the chat
that people gather for among the yams
and palm oils; the girls' new uniforms

for the school where they're just starting,
welcomes for the latest to come trudging
in, red-eyed. So far from what they've seen;
the casual dumped bodies of the slain

on sides of roads, jeep rumbling after jeep
and half-crazed boys, toting guns and dope –
though sometimes, gazing past the rain
that slants in through the window's broken pane

Kola's not so sure. Bustle at the counter;
all the talk this morning is of other
windows smashed in down the street
in Alimot's flat, where the women used to meet

to braid each other's hair. The night before
a letter shoved in underneath the door

warned Kola, *keep your monkey kids*
away from ours, we don't want your AIDS.

Kola keeps the letter, puts it at the back
of a high shelf with the others he got last week
after what happened down at The Green Lion.
Wallpaper peeling in the bar, the television on,

tuned in to Sky Sports; the locals' throaty roars
each time Andy Cole or Dwight Yorke scores.
How it started no one's sure, but what's certain
is the scar on Abayomi's face, nineteen

stitches in a crescent, lip to ear, from where
the glass went in, a stitch for every year,
and the whirr and hiss of those hospital machines
that Baku's still hooked up to. What this means

Kola doesn't know but there are other stories, other
nights as well; a beating for Popola in the chipper,
scuffles on the late night buses. And everywhere
the whispering; sly nudges, sullen stares

as they queue at the Department for a permit
or huddle in McDonalds, Pizza Hut,
or just gather on the corners of these streets
whose names they hardly know, unhappy ghosts

remembering the truckers thumbing notes as they
stepped into the ark of a container, or lay
beneath tarpaulin, waking to the grind of hawsers,
chains, another tongue, voices over water

as they docked, voices he can hear as afternoon
gives way outside to evening. Early moon.

The shut faces of the other shops.
Streetlights winkle on. Work stops,

footsteps hurrying past his doorway
heading home. Home, the footsteps say,
home through crowded streets, the walls
daubed with new graffiti, snarls

six feet high of rage and fear
go back where you came, we don't want you here;
home, the blinking monitors insist
as the last tube is removed from Baku's lifeless wrist

and Kola closes up the shop, his day finally over
as he walks into the night, hearing now a mutter
from the darkness; shadows step out, growing bigger
the last word a spat cherry stone: *go home, nigger.*

Watching Stars

for William

We cover miles together, you and I,
Rolling over the roads. You are
Sleep-suited, strapped in your child's seat,
An astronaut before blast-off.
Ahead of us the evening waits
For stars to emerge, as we do,
Watching the slate-blue sky until you

Are pointing suddenly amazed
At the first new far-off gleam
That gazes back at you. How near we seem
As I try to explain their distance,
Afraid of light years that must pass
Between us, space opening endlessly
In front of you as we drive towards

Darkened towns: the shops all closed, the schools
Silent. The empty insistent streets.
But you are asleep and dreaming now,
A glimpse of curls in my rear-view mirror.
Some day I'll look back to find you
Grown up and tugging at the handle,
Anxious to be gone

Into the night. The road ahead. And always
The stars, glinting above us
Like children from another time.
They whisper:
We have been here before memory and loss,
Our light remembered love and pain.
We see. And are watching still.

The Shipping Forecast

for my father

Tied up at the pier in darkened harbour,
the two of us below. The cabin's amber
light: me, surly in a sleeping-bag, fifteen,
and you past midnight, calmly tuning in
to the Shipping Forecast, long wave's
crackle, hiss, until you find the voice.
What's next for us: rain or fair? There are
warnings of gales in Rockall and Finisterre.
So near now, just this teak bulkhead
between us, and yet so apart, battened
hatches as another low approaches, the high
over the Azores as distant as a man is from a boy.
I think of my own boat one day, the deep.
Beside me the sea snores, turns over in its sleep.

from **Icarus Sees His Father Fly** (2004)

The Majestic

For This Week Only warned the message
in black marker on the latest glossy poster, as we
queued at The Majestic all those rain-filled afternoons
in the summer we discovered sex, and the ravages

of acne. More than the roar and flicker of the screen,
what mattered was what was happening here: wolf-whistles,
the footstamping and cheers from StarCrushed mouths as lights
went down, and we sat through the ads, the jerky newsreel,

Forthcoming Attractions on first dates, row on row
of one-armed crucifixions waiting for the action
to begin. High up, Fitzy – balding, tipsy – knocked back
one more shot as he loaded the projector and shambled down

to stand beside the swing-doors watching over us, a Zeus
in platform shoes. Cloud-eyed, we thanked God for the rain
skittering on streets as we turned, wet-lipped and full of purpose,
to each other amid the susurrus of sweet wrappings, urgent

fumblings in the mote-filled dark. We were young and scared
of nothing except heartbreak, the lasso of Fitzy's flashlight
twirling all around us as we struggled with zips and buttons,
groping towards the future with trembling clammy hands.

Rowing to America

I face backward to move forward; all I see
is stern, the muscled waves, wake's
disappearing vee. Under, swerve of silver,

fin-surge, stately boom, and under still
the seabed's prehistoric gloom. So long ago
the crowded pier, the reverie that led to where

I am now, neither there nor here, nothing of me left
except this seat splintering skin, these bloodied oars,
a memory of salt flesh as I haul in the line

again. Nothing. Gulls are watchful gods
as I saw sea beneath the clouds,
placing my trust in thole and bark

and dip my blades once more, pull up
a meteor shower of flying fish, thumping through
the spume-filled air then plunging back

into the foam – except for one, flipflipping
iridescence at my feet. Ancient scales; the little wings,
sturdy enough to bear a soul. And I devour it. Whole.

Chinese Lantern

The paper harbour twirled in the bulb's heat,
junks shimmering in the painted Shanghai night.
Over the frame stretched silk was sewn tight,
appliqued dragons and pagodas were sweet

inferences of flurried needles, thread,
bent heads, blur of finger and thumb
in a sweatshop at the back of some
boutique or bar, stitching until they bled

into red bolts of silk. Like flags the Orient
unfurled in our classrooms at Geography:
The Great Wall. Paddy fields. The muddied Yangtze.
A far-off place we struggled to invent

is still embroidered ornament. On the shelf
the light is solid, actual; an unco-opted gleam.
Teach me to tell image from pure beam,
to see what shines through instead: the thing itself.

Rhythm Painting

for Tony O'Malley

You heard it first, the lowing skies and roads
still smudges on a palette. Something is moving
under stone-crossed fields,
among the scrawn and scraggle of the hedges;
the breathing, pagan earth. The rain
a robe over the hidden land.
Easel angled to a dowsing stick, you divine this
rite of mud and bog in shade and hue,
hymn the crow-caw scoring the leaden air,
scratches on a canvas.

Elsewhere your brush hovers, landing in eleutheran light.
Each day a blur of distant music; earthlyre wings,
the hum of dreaming seas. Listening, you put on morning
in an impasto of turquoise, reds and blues,
watch moths gather over harvests standing stacked
against the evening; stooks of yellows, ochres, browns.
In the village they are wearing masks and flowers,
voices lilting into night. Ancient cadences,
rituals resonant in your rhythms of paint;
island songs, the occult earth-drummed rain.

A Carol

At midnight, the faint sound of a scuffle
High up on icy slates. Fantastic hooves
Wobble, trying to balance in the muffle
Of imagined snow on childhood roofs

Which, if fable, we invented for ourselves
As much as for the faces that peer after:
We thrill to tell of reindeers and of elves
That we may watch small eyes grow big, hear laughter

And learn again that what sustains the heart
Is not the proof, but wanting to believe
As we brighten dark days with stories of a start
That seems improbable, birth on a winter's eve

We sing of tonight, under the starry heaven
Waiting again for the miraculous to happen.

Where a Poem Comes From

The roof that I fell off when I was ten
was at the back of an abandoned house
I'd long been warned against, although

the thrill of loitering there,
deliciously illicit after school,
soon wore thin, a drama become casual

until the fall. What made me lose
my footing I don't know; carelessness,
day-dreaming or perhaps

pure chance shaping the drop
that left me on the ground
and roaring, pointing at my shin,

to where the rusted hidden spike
had entered in. My eyes filled with
the bloom and ooze of blood at first

but it was the later pain that mattered
more, a deep dull throb that seemed to be
just *there*, under bedclothes or school trousers,

the new skin forming and reforming as I
kept giving in to the urge to pick at it
again, with finger-nail or pencil-point,

hoping for the cruel vivid slash
so many TV baddies wore, but ending up
instead, I don't remember when

with a pale dent the shape
of a small flying fish, which made
my classmates smile. The house

is gone, lines of whitewash
rolled on tarmac, space to park
a hundred cars. And still I have the scar.

The Last Wolf in Ireland

Before, dark star of eagle; herds of elk
Lumbering through forests, gloom of oak

Hewn since by the acre, shipped to become
The ribs of abbeys and cathedrals, hum

Of parliament – their fists thumping the benches
Made from wood we'd marked as ours, stain of piss,

As they proclaimed the laws that soon would find us
Gasping in the ditches. Only the legends

Left behind: the stolen infant, suckled
Amongst cubs; the woolskin covering each pelt

While we moved stealthy through the dozing flock.
No mercy when we needed to attack;

An airy rush, fur tumbling to claw,
Muscle and sinew, our mouths rusting with gore.

Now I paw the undergrowth for carrion, snuffling
Beneath bushes, and watch the soldiers clanking

Into villages. Land being sheared and trimmed;
The new estates. Fire scented on the wind:

A country turned out, turning on its own as
Bounty hunters oil their muskets. Shadows

Over moonlit fields, the locals' silvered faces
Pointing out our sleeping young, the hidden places

They'll name after us when I am also gone
To earth among wing-feathers, antler bone,

The bog dreamtime; in black sod sunk below
Where no shone steel will ever fence or plough.

This Afternoon

Omagh, 15 August 1998

In Lingerie she is fingering a nightdress she might wear,
her two bridesmaids to-be skitting beside her. Elsewhere

schoolboys like disgruntled sheep wait in huddles
to be measured up for uniforms, dreaming of girls

and football, a new season this afternoon as summer ends
diminuendo in the town. Here is a father waiting for his sons,

a baby cooing in her pram, and two women browsing for a gift
as shopworkers count the hours down, not long left

till Saturday night, out for a few jars,
the raised TV set showing highlights in the bar

of games played earlier today by scrawny heroes,
the whole world at their feet, not much older

than the two who've just now parked the car, discreet,
that in a moment will bring them all together in the street.

Lindbergh Reaches Ireland

White knuckles on the joystick
in the frozen cockpit
half-dreaming of a brightly-lit oblivion.
Tries to hold eyes open with his fingers.
The last sandwich eaten,
across empty ocean 'Spirit'
rattles on, towards prayed-for headlands
The Three Sisters greening, and
a fisherman now lets go a wooden oar
to wave up at him astounded, seeing
America in his slipstream
sky a skein of vapour trails.

Nearing Distance

I keep your letters bound in red elastic;
no ribbon's silken finery of deceit. Each missive

strives for perfection, refusing irritably the bland,
that sly fifth column of the ordinary. Your rummage

incomplete, this is, you sigh, composed of only second-bests
and write of Paris, rues, the drifting suburbs. I feel

the lace of rain in my face on the Champs-Élysées.
Our intimate river's waters darken. Uneased, I

idle over notepaper, replay our favourite record.
The music bustles round me like a housewife

polishing each trace of you. Absence becomes silence.
I busy myself with the address, anticipate a future

correspondence: an envelope tumbling through the letter-box,
voices crackling over water. The minutes sidle by. In a

house outskirted by the hem of night-fall
you are tending children, drawing them towards bed-time

with a story. Undetected days slip past the clumsy cordon,
hatbrims dipped in an unhurried stroll. Maybe, you say,

we could meet up at Christmas. August is arrested;
the autumn's still curfews the evening. Is this

suspicion of a subterfuge a sign that we at last are
nearing distance, the amiable dilution of an intimacy?

The rubber band still holds, and we have sealed off all banalities, but it's time that's now ransacking our city, looting in doorways.

Judenbengel

In train-clatter he awakens from a dream
of Mama's strudel, waft of apples warming
in another summer kitchen. Sweet heart of marzipan

and bitter edge he still can taste, the cake
Hoffman had presented one Sunday afternoon,
new boots gleaming in the doorway as he enquired

for sister Anna. Leaning out the carriage-window
he can see red flags, the skewed black crosses at the centre
fluttering over villages, market squares massing

with uniforms, the bark and clip of drills. Further out
the opened ground, furrows newly turned for vegetables
like those he'd seen in Reinhold's. He'd loved

that grocery shop, loved when Reinhold allowed him
help out at weekends. Weighing and parcelling up.
The brisk song of the register until one day Reinhold

yanked him from the window and shoved him back
onto the store-room floor, emptying sackfuls of potatoes
over him, urging he keep quiet. Earthy dark, the tubers

all around him, a thousand silent skulls; Reinhold's twitter
at the counter as Hoffman screeched, demanding to know
where that *Judenbengel* was. Torch-loom: a door closing,

the soldiers stomping off into the street that would be littered
three nights later with the shards of broken windows,
glinting on the ground like fallen stars. Winter creeping in:

into the shut schools and cleared-out houses, frosting the signs
on benches in the park. Baleful trams; the hissing shops.
The evening a girl in ringlets spat in Anna's face, Mama opened

the school atlas, a map of Europe on the table while Papy
pulled the smallest suitcase from the wardrobe. "You're
a big boy now," he said. How to choose? Which toy,

which book, which photograph to pack inside
the little case that Mama, Papy must have known
even as they stuffed it full and snapped the catches shut

would hold a life? "But why me and not Anna; why not you?"
"She is older. We will join you soon. Promise you will write."
And he would tell them everything: the border guards, stolid

as Dutch Friesians; clamour of the seagulls at De Hoek as they
boarded the ferry, platoons of children hosting towards England.
Harwich in wet light; the sandwiches they'd chewed

in freezing summer beach huts, name-tagged, waiting
to be chosen: all this he would record in whorls of ink
on paper his house-mother gave him, letters home already

headed for oblivion, another hand stamping the familiar address:
Deported, Auschwitz. "Promise you will remember us."
As if he could forget the crowded midnight platforms, steam

belching from other trains already loaded for the East, and how
the tears came lumbering down Papy's cheeks, down Anna's
ashen face as he hugged Mama one more time, his own hot splashes

darkening the wool of her last coat, a stain spreading just below
the star she'd recently stitched on.

A Kite Lost in December

for John Shinnors

Here is the sound
Of wind and loss on canvas
Rushing in from sea
Past islands and lighthouses.
Over stubbled fields it comes,
A small high frame of colour
Tugged by unseen string
Towards this abandoned scarecrow town.
Listen: tonight it flutters in the streets,
It knocks against the boarded shops.
It taps for late drinks on the window
Of a pub closed twenty years ago.
The lovers and the children
Are gone, long gone,
Only the cats remain.
Under the bone moon they slink
Around the backs of houses
Beneath lines that wait for empty washing
In gardens that remember snowmen
With carrots for noses
And scarves to keep them warm.

This Child

And all these things were talked about through all the hill country of Judea; and all who heard them laid them up in their hearts, saying "What then will this child be?"
—Luke 1, 65–66

I. The Star

Nebula's slow blooming into flame
My birth, a thousand years before that night.
Meteors played dizzy astral games
Beneath Orion as I held high my light
Above caravans of souls, the icy hills,
That dusty kings, far off on raw-kneed camels,
Might see where they were headed. Up here
So many others, flaunting their own grandeur
As they jostled in the ether for their turn.
Why I was the one chosen to burn
More brightly than the rest I did not know,
But heard, through static, murmurings below,
The streets unsettled, new rumours of war
And others wondering what all this was for.

II. The Innkeeper's Daughter

Such a look my mother gave my father
When he turned those two away, though he was
Too busy to notice, wondering whether
He'd enough food to go round. Her urgent hiss:
"Go after them; tell them about the shed."
I ran out into the star-chilled evening
And caught them as they plodded up the road.
He was older, grave, but she was young, wincing
As the globe of the child inside her turned.
Across back fields I led them; already beasts
Were in, asleep, their breaths wreathing the fetid
Air. She was close, robes hoicked above her waist
When I went for help. Later, I brought back a rag doll
For the baby: I suppose I'd hoped it was a girl.

III. A Shepherd

I'd had a skinful earlier that night:
We'd all had, and who'd blame us, stuck out here
Freezing our balls off, the wolves and winter
Closing in. Whether that explains the light
I saw, or what I heard next, I can't say,
But the others saw it too, heard the voice
Telling us not to be afraid, good news
Happening in the town, a baby's cry.
More lights crowding the sky; we got going
Then, running just to get away as far
As we could, till I stumbled near a byre.
Inside a man distracted, cattle lowing,
A woman's sighs. So strange, and yet so right:
This swaddled child, the star above so bright.

IV. Joseph

Something so actual about a chair;
The honest, sturdy way it holds its ground
Among the off-cuts, shaving-curls. Furniture's
Reliable: you know just where you stand.
I can use a saw, make sense of wood,
Shape it to a bench, a press, a table,
And, up to this, worshipped one true god –
But who wouldn't now have doubts about it all?
First, her news before our marriage (the smirks
On neighbours' faces); then, the dreams began.
Along the slow trek south before the birth
I held her close, as if it were my own
In there, my life since never the same
As oozing onto straw, dazed, he became.

V. Herod and the Children

I know it sounds brutal, even bizarre;
It's not that I'd expect you to understand.
But such unrest; how else could I be sure
One king alone would rule this troubled land?
The business of the star did sound unlikely,
But why else those three would have made the visit
I don't know; as kings themselves, though, surely
They could see the need for order. Was it
Such a crime? It's a smallish town, remember;
So, seventy, say – or a hundred, maybe.
And how many would have made it past age two,
Mortality rates being what they were?
No, no bad dreams; I sleep like a baby.
You see, I just did what any man would do.

VI. The Camel Boy

Fine for the three of them, asleep in tents
Or the best rooms in each town that we'd pass through.
Outside we shivered, struggling to soothe
The moans of tethered beasts, and our own sense
Of fear on nights when that high star stared back
At us, reflected in our wide-eyed gaze.
A message came. In the gloomy palace
Staff were nervous, their king sullen, choleric,
Smiling hard as he insisted we return.
Or so the whispers said. By the time we'd come
To the right place, one animal was lame.
We unloaded inlaid caskets, brimming urns,
And waited by the fire. The snow still deep
When they came back; I swear I saw one weep.

Classics

Like elephants bemused by Alpine snow
we stumbled through histories of Greece and Rome
as Neddie Keane, a Hannibal from Ballina,
urged us daily on. We'd chant 'mensa',
sit through the grammar and the endless wars,
learning later how to skip off to serve Mass,
and afterwards quick nip of altar wine
among soutanes in the sacristy, O sacrament divine.
Ulysses amongst the Lotus-Eaters
had nothing on the nights we spent in Lysters
lined up for the swill, underage but hopeful,
fuzz-burned soldiers much too young for battle
until I'd wobble home at closing, tipsy victor,
to find my father in a god-like temper
stalking the house alone, demanding I tell
where on earth I'd been, although he knew full well,
and where did I think all of this was going.
And I would try to answer without slurring,
but what I meant just came out the wrong way,
the words so jumbled up and hard to say
that I may as well have talked to him in Greek,
more than the beer churning as I'd speak.

Injury Time

A mire, sad nets each Saturday; schools league. Game
over, home, I'd slump in worship: on the TV, news
of how *we'd* done today, West Ham, a London team;
'The Hammers', we aficionados liked to call
them. Here was where heartbreak began; the football
results, age twelve, wondering what they'd done to lose

to that crowd. Your crowd hardly ever seemed to lose
which didn't make things any easier, each game
Arsenal won one-nil "a victory for football",
you'd trump, as the announcer passed on the grim news.
Voice dropped a semi-tone in sympathy, he'd call
the numbers out that weekly threatened my esteem

for those boys in claret and blue, my chosen team.
But being a fan's about being loyal when they lose,
as well as win; a true vocation, like 'The Call'
priests heard, that we were all afraid we'd hear. The game
gave us an argot; sendings off, selection news,
who we're playing next. Back then, only football

counted, evenings in the garden banging the ball
again, again against the brick 'til you came home. "Team
spirit, lads; this is the one – I'm tellin' youse,"
urged 'Woodbine', our nicotine-stained coach, before we'd lose
once more, our dismal record streak of nineteen games
ended out of pity, a ref's dubious call:

another match you missed. Seasons later, when you'd call
I'd take up the role I'd learned from playing football;
defending deep, surprise attack the only game
I knew. I could name each year that East End team

won the Cup, but can't say when we started to lose
what should have mattered more between us than this news

we exchange instead, our answering machines in use
to record goals by Bergkamp, DiCanio, recall
how, though we'd started well, we still managed to lose.
Home wins, defeats; even the scoreless draws of football
draw us together now, like some hapless team
one–nil down, struggling for a goal to save the game,

knowing we're in injury time; knowing the next call
could bring the news that it's all over, the ball
gone dead. Knowing this game's one we can't afford to lose.

Icarus Sees His Father Fly

I've spent hours watching you
Glide, soaring on updrafts
Far above the wrinkled sea

And you nearly seventy!
Up there it's all wind and lift,
Wheeling in the brilliant blue

Harnessed in that brittle frame
Of feather, wood and gum.
You swoop with a delighted screech

And climb again, so high over the beach
You seem closer to the sun
Than me. But it's just one more game

To you, aloft on your own genius,
Showing how it's done.
I wonder did you ever doubt

Your own ability, trundling out
Off this cliff edge into the stun
Of that cool rush of nothingness

Beneath your feet? It's unlikely
You stopped first to think of reasons
Why you shouldn't also share the sky

With startled birds, clouds that grumble by;
All confidence, you said. I thought of gravity, some
Shift in the weather; breezes out at sea

Turning into sudden storms instead.
But you're drunk on air now, insistent
That I follow into azure by your side,

Making a man of me, or you ? So much I've tried
To make you proud. Shouts of encouragement
Loud in my head. Your voice once more. My arms spread.

Gam-Gam

Not even water with her whiskey – "there's enough in it already" –
on our visits to her parlour, Sundays fingering her piano
while the wireless murmured on. "Bullet-proof," my mother said:
two World Wars, nine Popes; so when she started getting our names
wrong we just giggled, playing the parts of those other
    grandchildren,
oblivious to my father's frown. "They'll never take her out alive,"
he shook his head in the car after as we drove back to town, away
from the old gunslinger, whiskery in a twin-set, holed up in her
    hideout

waiting for the law — who came immediately, it must be said, in
    answer
to her call that all her jewellery had been stolen, the fresh-faced
    one
bemused to find at last the glistening stones at the back of a high
    shelf,
stuffed inside a teapot she seldom used. In November, after leaf-
    fall,
she fell twice. On Christmas Day at dinner her voice shook a
    little fist
at my young brother, some imagined slight over the roasties,
    turkey breast.
We sulked as birthdays passed, unmarked by cards enclosing
    fivers: how
could she forget us, yet remember who had danced with who on
    summer nights,

the time the turning of a card had for one man meant the boat,
    and
so many of their names: the latchikoes and skelpers, go-by-the-
    walls;

even the runty dog she'd loved, fifteen years dead, who she still called
for hours at twilight in her garden while the doctor phoned my father
to explain. "Thinning of the brain," he said, "there isn't any cure. You'll need
to keep an eye on her." Which we did, watching as she sailed away, a liner
in the darkness, the lights on board one by one going out. So that when
she turned up in her night-dress at the supermarket, where she fell for the last time,

she was beyond the gaze of neighbours at the checkout, ascending the ramp
of the ambulance as if it were a scaffold, and beyond us too, the hurry
of my father to the hospital after they'd told him she was sinking fast.
Parched flowers. The steel-framed bed. And him, still trying to work out
what was happening in her head as she turned from some horizon
to ask him who he was, her eldest son: "It's me; it's me, Gam-Gam,"
scaled to a mote in her blank stare, his voice catching at the moniker
for Grandma our childish tongues once stumbled on.

The Loss

You are everywhere I look about this house,
Hiding under chairs or around doorways,
Longed for like a small chance missed

Imagined yet. Giggles from an empty corner;
That bump behind the drapes a wind
Gusting through a broken pane. This is

The still life of your absence, etched
In silence. Ashes in the grate are unsung names
For you; the bowed heads of flowers

Bright bedroom colours I'll unpick
From a vase in the bay window
That today is framing swollen hills and

Clotted darkening streams, the winter
You leave after, a shadow gone through
A gap in the fence only a child could fill.

Butterflies

This evening, nothing unusual
About this bed-time ritual,
Nothing cleaner or more palpable

Than your delighted shrieks and splashes
As you hammer bathwater, all purpose
Or pour cupfuls over upturned toys,

Submerged, helpless. Later you burrow
In the bedclothes, wood creature before winter
While darkness gathers at the window.

The door's pulled to; one last sly creak.
Thieves in our own house, we speak
In whispers, creep upstairs once more to check

On you, then fall asleep until your sudden cry
Hauls us from bed in the small hours, and we
Come trudging, slightly stunned, the way

Others in another time went, herded onto trains
Their children immaculate, holding hands,
Wild eyed, afraid of where the line would end:

Concrete and wire. Watchtowers. Each day
They filed into the yard, silently
Gaunt rumours of death. *Arbeit macht frei*

The soldiers said, free as the butterfly
That once, just once, a young boy
Saw flit over the fence from fields nearby,

Grace-note from a loved remembered tune
Jinking about him in the dizzying sun.
Then, a soul rising, the butterfly was gone

Disappearing into hazy distance
Like childhood memories. Innocence.
That boy is dead long since

But you are here, cherished and suckling
On a bottle. Outside the world is waiting
To bring on another summer morning,

Birds fussing in the trees.
Soon the sky will fill with butterflies,
Their wings dappling the air, ease

And flutter, lilt of a child's song
That breaks the heart in two and then is gone.

The Match

in memoriam J.F.

for *Paddy*

The doors and boot banged shut, the engine not
yet started and you'd be switching on. "He hits it
long again." How many Sundays did we hear
a high ball arcing through a summer sky before

being plucked out and belted back into the maw
of our car, among chocolate stains and crisps, more
toothsome fizz-filled drinks than we could finish?
"A right shemozzle here," O'Hehir in the Yiddish

screeching with excitement, my young brother and I
trading pinch for pinch in the back seat as we
headed for the shore, hoping the rain would finally get bored
with us, drift off to ruin someone else's day. You'd

always drive, though you were nowhere near
the spattered windscreen. Eyes fixed in a beatific stare
beyond Strand Road, the seagulls hanging round like knives;
all you could see were goals and points and wides,

Micheàl's frenzied commentary yammering non-stop
from the speaker. Even when you'd park you'd keep
the spell, carrying a transistor over still-damp sand,
a tabernacle tuned in to Athlone, the same one I'd

collected after from the hospital, with the rest of your things.
I'm turning the dial now, following the wave-bands
in case I'd find you. But the only sound I hear is the soft hiss
of the sea. In the end you bowed your head, the way you'd always

done at Mass, but on those Sunday afternoons gave thanks and praise for hurling and football; me a sherpa stumbling behind, lugging bath-towels and a deckchair as you strode ahead to join the congregation, stretched out beside battered radios along

the beach or in the dunes until "The final whistle …" tinny cheers of far-off crowds rising above us like hosannas in the air.

Sea Language

I was seven when you first taught me
The language. *Halyards. The mast.*
Mainsheet. Boom. You'd hoist
Those words above us, proudly,

As if you'd made them
Specially for me. Our house
Was a ship full of sails and shouts,
The rattle of rigging, and you at the helm,

A voice that was always there
Even after gales and waves had died.
I can still hear you inside
A harbour bar, ashore somewhere,

Talking up a storm while I
Shivered and drank Cokes until I almost burst.
Now, beer-bellied, I can taste
The salt you left, and keep a weather eye

The way old sailors do.
Our lives together have been distances,
Arguments over routes, directions,
Which way the wind really blew;

The usual son and father stuff.
These days I prefer squalls to the silences
In the wary talk of sea between us,
Afraid of when our craft won't be enough.

The Grip

Later, on a summer's evening, we drive out
to my father's club to play. "It's time you took up
golf," he says, meaning that it's time I spent
less time in the pub. We park among the sleeping

chrome and head for the first tee. Swathes of green
and figures clustered everywhere, but all I can see
is my father as he steps up to plant the ball: a pause
and then he hits off neatly; short, but straight and true.

My turn. I draw a sword from the borrowed bag
and wait. "The club is an extension of yourself,"
he reminds. I feel the five-iron go limp in my hands.
"Don't try to hit too far too soon." I am going to show

him and the watching world; I am going to smash
this ball onto the moon. Blood-thunder; the club-head
hurtles past. I gaze hopefully a hundred yards ahead
then back down at my feet: the ball, unmoved, still there.

This is called 'a fresh air'. Another go; the ball squirts
twenty yards out left. Already I am struggling to keep up,
listening to the same advice I seem to have
been hearing all my life: *Take it easy.* Instead of getting

closer I am further away than ever, slashing and
hacking through scutch grass, or looking for a ball
I'll never find in the deep rough: in trouble everywhere.
Keep your head down. He's out on the fairway,

alone; I can hear the small clean thwock as he swings
and follows through, repeating, the same thing,
mechanical, unrelenting, like the arguments
we have each time we meet. Hummed snatches

of Sinatra as he waits for me to join him, so distant still.
Go back slowly. I am counting once again the atrocities
of our wars, the years of peace that might have been
now lost to us as surely as those dimpled spheres

long forgotten, nesting in the gorse. The light fading,
he turns to me: "Let's finish here." He bids me come
out from the weeds and thorns, and I do, ending up
beside him on the edge. He plops a new ball

down, then steps behind and puts his arms round me.
I feel his hands closing over mine. *Try holding it
like this.* The club purrs, lofts the ball into the dusk.
So close then, the two of us; almost close enough to kiss.

from **On Water** (2014)

Wilson

Years after all that, we're still out playing,
still together. I'm longer than him now;
now he complains his game is breaking down.
We both know what this means. Ahead, I wait

for him to make up ground between us, and grip
the club the way he showed, my thumb across
the maker's name: *Wilson*. Breathless
when he reaches me, he eyes my hands:

"You're holding on too tight." Is this
his way of saying goodbye, or just bustle,
the golfer's artful chatter designed to unsettle?
Either way, it works: up close, where it matters

he's all lobs and flops and lovely pitches, soft hands
that once saved the lives of stricken children
and still have what they call 'the touch'.
I stab and chop, my ball careening past the target

first from one side, then the other while he
rolls his sweetly up to stop. "Getting nearer,"
he consoles. The flag flutters above the cup
but I'm thinking of the other hole, the opened

ground where we'll all finish. His ball
just inches from the drop. Our lives together
a groove worn by my thumb. The *Wil* of Wilson
almost gone; soon all that will be left will be the *son*.

When Grumpy Met Lindy

Where I grew up they used to say
if you saw a car going round the streets
with no one driving it, that was him,

my grandfather. A pin-striped pocket battleship
patrolling the out-trays for forty years
in the Department, among the sniggerings

of nylons and Brylcreems who gave him the name
Grumpy, he looked only ahead and even now
would chide me for glancing over my shoulder,

feeling him close by as I go back
to 1936 when Charles A. Lindbergh,
'Lucky Lindy', came to Ireland for three days

and stayed for ten. A brown sea: hats at the aerodrome.
De Valera terrified, buttoned up for his first flight,
and Lindy, dapper in a suit and goggles, smiling

for the cameras, wondering when this November fog
would lift enough for him to head for home. Grumpy's
in a trilby, waiting in a line with the rest of the officials

to shake the hand of Lindbergh. His hand's outstretched,
the same hand that would later slip a coin for sums
well done or words spelt out correctly, that I might learn

the benefit of industry in addition to its virtue. Here
comes Lindy. The first man to fly the Atlantic
on his own! And I see the hand holding the stick,

head lifting up and up into the air until his grip
suddenly loosens, and my grandfather falls
beside his brand new walking stick in our back garden

before I can discover what he'd said, if anything,
when they finally came face to face; a mumbled
greeting lost in clouds of breath, perhaps, or even just

the grin I'd settle for myself as I stretch out
my hand as far as it will go,
hoping I might touch a hero's wing.

from *Rare Birds*

Lyrebird

His hoard of shiny things the songs of others:
honeyeater, cockatoo and kookaburra
but less an artful thieving than a helpless ear
as now he sings out, innocent and exact

the whirr of camera-shutter, the rising grind
of chainsaws getting closer in rainforests of Australia
on the far side of the world, though nearer
than the southern seaside town we stayed in

every summer where my sister, aged thirteen
and already mad for road, spent all her days
loitering with intent among 'the Willie boys',
Dillon and McCarthy, their arses worn away

from propping up street corners, and hit back
when taunted by me as to which one was her lover
that I was nothing but 'a langer', the Cork appendage
brandished by her in perfect sing-song pitch.

Roll Call

Andrews *whose pimples earned the nickname 'Pizzaface'*
Byrne *who left school early with two uniformed police*
Cosgrove *who rented out his brother's porno mags*
Daly *who sells pre-owned Beemers, Mercs and Jags*
Earley *who always wanted something more from life*
Farrell *who ran off with the history-teacher's wife*
Galvin (deceased) *who never learned to swim*
Hughes *who got five years for that pension investment scam*
Irwin *who in science class blew up a spotted toad*
Jackson *who blew up a crowded shop on the Kings' Road*
Kilroy *who carved his name on every single desk*
Lynch *who once at 4am was dealt a Royal Straight Flush*
Malone *who despite everything turned out all right in the end*
Neilan *who still would sell his soul to have one friend*
O'Toole *who at the last count had fathered seven kids*
Power *who had recently the operation to become Ms.*
Quinn *who always hated any kind of football*
Reynolds *who so nearly won a bronze Olympic medal*
Sullivan *who would not believe what he could not see*
Tobin *who tested positive last week for HIV*
Usher *who, before he kicked it, drank away two pubs*
Valentine *who at his ninth attempt became captain of the golf club*
Wall *who was Head Boy and is now Third Sec in China*
Xavier *who was an altar boy and is now a Hare Krishna*
Young *whose antics in a pool brought down the Government*
Zee *who was then, is now, and always will be absent.*

The Clock Tower

Rung by rung we climbed, ascending into what seemed
a kind of heaven, the school's clock tower strictly out of bounds,
the pleasure in the lung-constricting terror, knowing the fall
would kill us. But we knew little else, and dying was so far off,
further than the dizzying football fields, the cars below like toys,
the matchbox houses lighting one by one the autumn evening,
and beyond all this the sea, clutching her frozen souls.
We were immortal then, untidy ink-stained gods
watching from on high, above time's granite certainties,
the steel hands of the clock face like all schoolboys
never quite telling the truth, but set instead a little fast,
as if what lay ahead for us would not come soon enough.

Triptych

Blown out in a gale
discarded brollies, flapping
like exhausted bats.

*

Cherry blossoms strewn
outside the women's shelter.
Last year's confetti.

*

Thumped leather rising
high over the frosty pitch;
a muddy star.

Amendoeira

I love this story my mother told me:
the Moorish prince who falls in love
and marries a girl from the far north.
He brings her home. The palace marvels:
her skin of ivory, her wheaten hair; her slivers
of sapphire streaming sadness. She misses
her own home, and most of all she misses
snow. And so, because he loves her and cannot
bear to see her cry, the worried prince commands
that every field be planted with amendoeira,

trees of almond blossom. The young princess
shrugs, resumes her bathing in the pool
of her own misery, hating the scent of musk,
the rustling silks, the fat-faced watchful maids.
A season passes, and another, and then early
on a breezy day in spring the prince bids
his heart-sore princess come to the window
that she may see the snow his love has made
for her, a blizzard of pink blooms falling
across the land. And here the story ends

or should do: the princess weeping, this time
with joy; the prince beside her gazing proudly
at the laden boughs. But what happens next,
I want to ask: how does love survive the empty
limbs, the fleshy drifts becoming rust ?
And then my mother brings me to the window,
pointing to the tree planted so long ago,
the tree my own children are shrieking under now,
hurling armfuls of blossoms at each other,
and my father, still shaking the branches.

Poetry

for Conor O'Callaghan

The dark nights at the driving range.
The early starts, sun singing off the dew.
The shudder, standing up to open ground
On the first tee. The many ways of being wrong:
Hooked. Sliced. Topped. Shanked. Pulled.
The floundering for hours in bunkers
And still not getting out. The lost balls.
The prizes everyone else wins. The drinking.
The yardage, working out how far to go.
The ones that start off looking great but end up
Short. The shots that try to do too much. The know-alls.
The two-foot putts that you still miss. The yips.
And – sometimes – the little click when things go right:
The sweet sound that keeps you coming back.

Team Photo

One joker up on tiptoe at the back;
centre, the proud captain, holding ball. Arms
folded in a swagger, we were ready

for anything the world could hurl at us.
Pirate beards, teen-idol hair – the glamour:
we were sure to knock 'em dead

in the bar after. Boots crusting with pitch-muck
and tradition; the jerseys that on fired-up afternoons
we'd sworn we'd die for. And (not in picture)

the all-in-this-together of it, lingering here
like the reek of Deep Heat in the changing room
as players take the field to scattered cheers.

Shakespeare in Ireland

One bearded me, hop-addled, the hour late;
a rug-haired kerne, grog-blossoms in full bloom.
"What business have you here?" The age-old hate
glittering in those bane-filled eyes; the room
full suddenly of music, flute and fiddle,
as snag-toothed locals gaily take the floor,
advance, retreat, advance, rehearsing battle;
a merry dance they led us. But what for?
A charnel-house, this place: rain-lashed, hag-cursed,
a song that's sung shut-eyed against the pain.
There is no future here, only the past;
a blood-revenant, come to avenge the slain,
who'd this night gladly kill me, one brute blow
as jigs and reels come rivering off the bow.

Beads

When the wire-ends pricked our fingers, the sisters
urged we think of Jesus, and how little was our suffering
by comparison. We threaded bead on bead to make
a decade at a time of our time here, ten years gone
along with songs we sang in choir, as if
our soaring voices could lift us also upwards
to that other world from where the swan had come
crash-landing in the yard, off-course, beautiful and stunned
before taking fright and taking off again, wings
still beating in our ugly-duckling hearts. We made
Our Fathers and Hail Marys, Glory Bs and wondered
where our own mothers might be, and what we had
done wrong to end up here, standing in a line
on freezing mornings, our sodden bed-sheets
draped over our heads, unholy ghosts who saw
through tear-scald and the wet stench of ammonia
the other, darker stains of older girls
and were afraid of where we next would bleed.

Skellig

The night the Abbot died all the book-satchels
fell down, their psalters scattered over the stone floor
like ransacked towns. I could feel Flann's bony knee

pressed close, too close to mine as we gathered in to pray,
the oratory an upturned boat, and we twelve souls the crew,
marooned out on this rock. "Never can we hide

from the Divine," intoned the doleful Malachy, already bristling;
the importance of new office. I bowed my head and wondered
if He could see the claw of Flann's right hand, rummaging

underneath his habit, or how Aodh quaffed as always
a little too much wine from the battered chalice. Outside stone huts
huddled in the gale, two rows of rough-cut crosses in the graveyard

a mouth of broken teeth as we prepared the body, muttered
supplications to forgive the dead man's sins. Will He also
forgive Fionan, prayers on sunny days forgotten as he dozes

amongst sea-pinks and the daisies; or vain Cellach in the garden,
swagger of the hoe he handles better than any other man;
or Aeneas, swearing by the names of all the saints

that this portly sad-eyed puffin trembling in his hands
was really more fish than fowl, whose flesh we thus
could safely eat on Fridays? And will He also forgive

other carnal pleasures? Before this, back on land,
bells tolled as monks warned of the devil's many forms;
how the young girl I'd watched working in the scullery

could be the shape of evil. Head down, pert rump up,
her hands were small birds fluttering among the tunics
and the scapulars. One loosened strand of hair dangled

from her cap like a dark question. *"You have answered
the call of God,"* the elders rasped, *"who asks you serve him
somewhere else instead, away from all temptation."* Now I

lay down my days in dry stone walls, and kneel on clouds
to set into the cliff the steps we build, rising from the cove,
each slab a prayer ascending into heaven. We plant

celery and parsnips, and stake our faith in this high place;
no frost or plague can reach us, and even the bravest longship
fears to cross these widow waves. I know the cry

of kittiwake and razorbill, the time of every tide,
and on clear days can see south to the Bull Rock, and the Cow,
but know as well I'll never see again that little maid

who comes to me in dreams in my dark cell. Some night
I'll stiffen in my sleep for the last time. And then? And then?
The greatest sin of all the sin of doubt: that all there is

is all we leave behind; crude annals, the sound
of callused hands working stone. *Matins. Lauds.* We count
the hours on knotted cords, keep vigil for gentle Muredach

until dawn, pink light blooming on the arch
of Needle's Eye and on the stations, a *via Crucis*
hewn from wind and rock. I'll offer up

these blistered fingers aching for fond caress,
and press my lips instead against this wooden cross,
praying that my sins may fall from me like tears.

The Volta

Ireland's first cinema, opened in 1909 by James Joyce

A gleam, this new idea in his head:
a chance of turning coin, his city still
in blackness, awaiting sound and light

so he comes back, acquires a hall
off Sackville and fills it; wooden
benches, Windsor chairs for the quality

a carpet sticking its red tongue out
along the centre aisle, potted palms
beside the orchestra, and a screen

and opens in December, frost and ice
and snow that soon would be
general all over Ireland

counting heads, the queue outside
curious under gaslight;
then curses the bad weather as the stream

dries to a trickle, the money
running out, and closes six months later
the doors locked and the posters

gone, but not the taste for it.
How well he knew us
as we crowd in once again

loving the womb-warm inky dark,
the press of flesh, and stories stories
stories created out of all of us, pictures

alive in flame-flicker, a huddle around
cave paintings made from the crushed
bones and blood of the animals we painted.

Dick The Younger

As a boy he lured strays into the yard
with purloined titbits of offal they all fell for,
the condemned mongrels struggling to escape

as the cord tightened on the gibbet Johnny Appleseed
had sworn he'd seen him making, though Mary Parr
was doubtful, and Ellen Cooper shook her head of wheat

saying it had been fashioned by his father, who
like his son had one cast eye, as if a part of him
could not bear witness to the dark art of his office,

an heirloom grimly handed down. Though crops failed
his tree bloomed all year round, dangling
from its single branch our whole town's rotten fruit,

utterers and cutthroats, murderers and highwaymen
we'd thrill to watch being hoist, their boots kicking the air
in a last polka: 'Sweet' William Webster, who stole a ewe,

grinning his idiot grin as he slowly climbed the scaffold,
and Widow Howcroft, who poisoned seven babies,
screeching obscenities in the shadow of the rope,

the knot that Dick The Elder had learned from his own father,
who'd likewise grumbled at the cost of ladders, and had known
in a handshake a felon's counterweight; thirteen hitches,

and an eye the rich and poor could pass through. That winter
the fever came for Mary, the Divine Lord deciding
fourteen summers was enough, and in the springtime

Dick The Younger came for me, clutching shyly
a posy of snowdrops, the blooms already dead. "As well him
as another," my mother said, who worried I was plain,

though I'd have chosen Johnny Appleseed, by whom Ellen
bore ten children. And I bore one: this wall-eyed child cradled
beside me, who in time will learn to bargain with the Crown

over expenses, who soon will set our sinners dancing
to his tune, and whose small fist closing tight around
my finger may yet weigh me for the drop.

Kecksies

"As good as any lad" – my father, swallowing, anxious for
the shilling. The stranger then: *"She'll do."* I walked behind him
    from the market
as he pointed with his ashplant to fences and the river,
and swollen-uddered cattle in the pasture, waiting. His wife's eyes
on my hips as she led me to the milking shed, and I knew
she was a field no seed would grow in. The beasts came easy
as I squeezed the way my late mother had shown. Churns

filled: a bumper yield. He came easy too, when we lay down
amid the lowing and the shuffling of hooves. My belly swelled.
He promised me the top field, the smallest cow, but one night I
    heard her
soused, asking him where I'd go once they'd got the baby,
and he tapped the ashplant and said river. My mother showed me
something else as well: how to find them in the ditches, amongst
docks and thistles, the white flower and rank leaves which meant

the bad seeds she called kecksies. Next day I tied the little heifer
and drove the others to the river, watching as they tumbled
    ullulluing
into the dark water. I laced each brimming churn, and seasoned
with those husks a parsnip sauce for supper, imagining them
    both
suddenly struck dumb among the dishes, their bodies slumped
like sated children in their chairs. On the road I whispered to the
    heifer
and listened to the grass in the top field. Inside the kecksie stirred.

Lamp

i.m. Caroline Walsh

Before cave-paintings there were caves,
wretched places, cold and damp and dark,
and although they built fires at the entrance,
and gathered round in skins to eat the burnt flesh
of slain deer, and kept watch for sabre-tooths
and ravenous bears prowling the ice wastes,

they were afraid to look behind, back
past the shadows into the blackness
of the deepest reaches of those walls
where no one dared to go without a light,
and all those bulls and stags and horses
would have stayed inside the small brains
of the hunters unless one of the tribe

had not taken a sandstone slab, and slowly
hollowed out in it a space for deer-fat
and a sprig of juniper as a wick, and kept it lit
so that the painters, and the others,
could see what they were making;
fabulous beasts, whinnying and prancing
and pawing the ground, alive
in the guttering flame of a careful lamp.

from *Last Orders*

The Upstairs Bar

i.m. Paddy Hunt

After we've searched all the usual haunts
someone suggests we try The Upstairs Bar,
a new place, on the main street, sandwiched between
a chi-chi restaurant and a wound-down video store

in this village where you've long time been
the unelected mayor, and here you are, practising as ever
the art of conversation, thrust and parry, to and fro,
and all the while an ear cocked and a weather eye

for nuggets of gossip, tittle-tattle to add to your collection,
gems you'd feign at first a pantomime reluctance to show us
before relenting, dropping gleefully each bright new stone
into the pool, then sitting back to watch the ripples spread,

and so much else stored up there, in the attic of this house
we close the door and turn the key on; tax wheezes and the tunes
of all the songs, the last word on everything and a word
for everyone, the mighty and especially the fallen,

willing to go a bit of any road except the road for home,
and a place too in your shy heart for children, who sensed
your sense of mischief that would surely have had you
sniggering with delight in the course of your own funeral

at the stern warnings from the pulpit on the evils
of double-parking in church grounds, and the delicious,
knowing praise of your 'support for local industry' delivered
to pews filled with long-faced barmen, the queue of sympathisers

stretching back to Cork and Sligo, the length and breadth
of this island which seemed sometimes too small for you,
the air hostesses three parts charmed, one part bemused
as you sipped lethal gin and tonics the whole flight,

and if the Buddhists have it right maybe you'll fly back
one day as a parrot, landing on the shoulder of a clutch
of balding legal eagles and other quare hawks, where you'll
squawk once more in protest at their feeble-minded drivel,

but if it's The Upstairs Bar instead it'll be a fine place
to walk into and find you, soaking up the atmosphere,
as you turn with a smirk, and a quick rub of the beak to say
glint-eyed, conspiratorial, "I shouldn't be saying this."

Raindrop

This you know: the muffled drumbeat
singling out your window, diamond
on the glass; or, from a sullen cloud
a pearl on your lapel dissolving, a dark wound.

Now look again: this cradling of light
suspended from the edge of leaf is like
the swaddled infant dangling from the beak
of the stork that brought new babies when we

were young and could not understand.
One last time, while there's still time to see
me and you, the garden where we stand,
our world shrunk to this gleam

the slightest shudder would let fall.
Into a cupped hand which may not be there at all.

What They Carried

Sometimes a brimming trunk lugged miles
past smashed-in cabins, empty rills, ditches
clotted with the dead, but mostly
a life bundled in a blanket;
gansies, shawls, a pot and spoon,
a bauble for the baby not yet born

or whatever they stood up in,
darned petticoats and fraying trousers,
a hat jammed on a head teeming
with dreams and busy lice, the typhus
travelling with them to the fever shed
at King Street, the lazy beds of Cabbagetown

dozens buried at a time, their last rite
a shovelful of lime. They braced themselves
against the lurch of ocean and the future
and vowed to keep the faith they'd never lost,
despite all this, in a merciful Almighty
who watched them as they clambered up
through narrow hatches, down on to the dock
to stand shivering, exhausted in new light;

who listened always, they insisted,
to their whispered supplications
that what they carried with them
might be equal to these streets
already greening to new leaf
and what they'd left behind
or thought they had. Clay
under their fingernails. Their grief.

On Water

(i) A Wedding Guest

We stayed just outside Cana, which is actually
a very pretty town, although the military
seemed to be everywhere. The weather on the day
was perfect – I wore my new papyrus shoes –
and the bride looked absolutely radiant
(her dress cost a small fortune). They did choose
to serve the best wine last, after a slight delay
but the customs they have here are different,
as Zach explained. Still, it did seem rather odd,
as did that young man (the woman by his side
his mother, I believe) who spoke to the stewards;
so quiet and assured as they fussed over the ewers.
The group with him were whispering about a sign.
A rough lot, they were. But the wine tasted divine.

(ii) The Basket

I heard them mutter as they counted heads
that this was madness, how there'd never be
enough even to go around themselves,
never mind the rest of us. We could see
the darkness rolling over the sand
and huddled close together, watching him.
A dog barked. A child who could not understand
her hunger cried. I thought again of home,
so far away, so many of us here
with so little to go on. Then the voice,
his murmured blessings rising in the air,
rustles as the wicker passed along. My hands
plunged in: warm bread; fish scales, the tang of sea.
The basket was as deep as Galilee.

(iii) The Storm

We should have seen it coming, I suppose,
but we were dog-tired when we left, and skies
seemed clear, the sun's work done, sinking astern.
He'd flaked out down below, missing his turn
to steer - and who could blame him, wanting peace
from days of heat and dust, and everywhere
excited hordes, clamouring for a piece
of him. A shame to wake him, but we were
in real trouble, too late to shorten sail,
heaving waves swamping the decks, boom of gale
enough to raise the dead. I slapped his face:
"We're going down! Don't you care?" He blinked, then stared
as if he'd come back from another place
to wind and water, waiting for his word.

(iv) Baptist

But no one knew from where. Feral, hairy,
his beard alive with insects, streaks of honey;
that stinking hide! And wounded, wounding eyes
urging repentance on the restless queues
as we lined up to take the plunge. Hawkers
selling song-birds, dates and sherbets; raucous
warnings of sandal-thongs, the everlasting fire
until they met. Awe, perhaps, or fear;
his voice a quiver as he beckoned him wade out
to where he stood. Hands cupped over the bowed
head; a river falling through his fingers. Dove?
No. No voice; no heavens opening above
except after: rain, long prayed for, from blue skies
like sudden small clear blessings on our lives.

(v) Jairus

One with him shook his head: "*You can't buy this*" –
although I could see the other two were
keen to haggle, see how much more I'd give,
as if there was some price I would not pay
to bring her back. To see my daughter live.
A swarm around him, pawing at his robes
and he was weary, wheeling with a sigh,
"Alright, alright". Dark room; her husk. Choked sobs
when he pronounced her sleeping, urging her
to rise. The same as all the rest, I thought:
the rhetoric, the empty promises;
I'd *wanted* to believe, you understand,
as he called for water. The cup lifted
to lifeless lips. And then she touched his hand.

(vi) On Water

I'd seen it happen years ago, back when
he was just a child; couldn't have been more
than eight. I'd warned him: stay close to the shore,
don't go deeper than your knees. But even then
he had this way of doing what he thought was right.
My back was turned – his baby sister, red-cheeked
in the heat – and he was gone. I panicked;
ran down to the edge, screamed his name in fright
until I saw him, going out with the tide
walking on water. Little splashes as
he skipped from wave to wave; astonished fishes
leaping underneath his feet. Arms stretched wide,
he smiled back, showing how easily it was done.
Which it was, compared with what was yet to come.

The Wave

in memory of those who perished in the Fastnet Yacht Race 1979

Grizzled mainsail trimmer off a Yankee clipper
the only one to call it, cloudless August morning
in the shore-side caff. "Something big

out there in the Atlantic," southern drawl amid
Sweet Afton, waft of last night's beer, bitching
about skippers over eggs and bacon. Tinkling

masts. The gleam and spank of sail, yachts prancing
in the harbour, courses plotted for The Rock. No runic
satellite, no merry weather-man could then foretell

the mangled spars. The drifting empty hulls.
The sodden bodies hauled aboard by trawlers;
the others, never found, lists taped up in windows

near the greasy spoon where that old salt had seen
what Hokusai saw, beyond the geishas and the fishmarkets
of Edo, his own floating world as he leaned over

a wood-block carved from cherry to make his picture
of the wave off Kanagawa: out of nowhere, a rumble
in the ocean, foam-flecked surge gathering in the arc

of its own rage into a roar of water, brute beauty
trembling above the wooden sampans, the cowering men.
Poised. Ready to sweep everything away.

The Ark

Past the sign that offers WIGS FOR RENT
at Minihan's the chemist, who still complains
of rivulets of stout dribbling down into his shop;
then in under the arch through which a man might ride

a horse, and up the stairs, the same stairs Eddie Guest
once stumbled on, and fell, and sued, and lost. A door
opening into an interior by Vermeer: light falling
from a window on the left, lambent on the counter;

the figures perched on high stools nursing pints and chasers.
The sense that some small thing is just about to happen
here, where anything is possible, where merchant princes
wait their turn and Bernie Murphy, sandwich-board-man,
     becomes

a city councillor. And you, mein host, presiding, gazing out
across the bar at new arrivals before you amble over to pour
another splash of what you've always loved to call 'a talent
to abuse', a talent nurtured in another time when Select Bar

meant no fools ever suffered, no interruptions tolerated to quiet,
courteous drinking. The legends grew: how once, when he refused
to remove it, you snipped off with a scissors a patron's garish tie;
how tourists seeking merely coffee or a soft drink were briskly
     shown

the door. Word was, nobody was anybody in this town
until they'd been barred by you, though at times the person
you most wanted to get rid of was yourself, your own best
     customer,
dank afternoons alone when the smoke-stained wooden panels

closed in around you like a coffin and you sank down to the dregs,
down to the ocean floor at the bottom of your glass. "Quit
    drinking,"
said the doctor, "quit, while you're ahead." "Who says I'm ahead?"
the return from the baseline, proving you can always tell a
    Corkman,

but you can't tell him much. Some day the Lee's green waters
will rise to swallow up all of these streets; Patrick Street, and
    Winthrop,
and this street too; Oliver Plunkett, our favourite bloody martyr,
but when the deluge comes if anything survives it will be this place,

an ark filled with chairs and tables from another turn-of-century
    ship,
the picture signed by Einstein and the letter from Cole Porter,
    and forty
days and nights of classical and jazz and opera, enough even for you,
a balding Noah in bi-focals, still humming Shostakovich and
    insisting

on good manners as the denizens stare out upon the lost world
floating past, clinging on to Bernie Murphy's sandwich-board.

Scrimshaw

for M

Among the twisted innards, shock of crimson
he found this: a pause, mid-flense, to tuck
into the pocket of the leaky oilskin he'd

be drowned in later the little stumpy tusk,
a hundred in that fearsome head, a tooth
for every cask of viscous ooze becoming

suds lathering a widow's hands, or oil soaking
through wick, the hurricane lamp flickering
beside him, nights on deck, on watch,

boards sagging under the leviathan dead,
etching, scratching out as I do now
this story: clouds and masts, the tiny whaler

following through waves a plume of foam
engraved on this keepsake I make that you
may keep when I am all at sea, so far

from home and so much water as I
chase down the latest poem that briefly surfaces
off starboard to shouts, quivering blades

before descending once again into
the unfathomable, a deep darker than ink
or any marks I might set down tonight,

creak of moonlit rigging, the songs of long-dead
sailors carrying on a wind up from the south,
salt gust on these chapped lips that long for yours.

The Blue Man

Hulk of ferry, scream of gull; the Irish Sea
behind in darkness, shaking her grey head.
Pasty-faced in platform's sodium glare, we hefted
rucksacks and suitcases, plastic bags of duty free,

the clunk and clink of grog and cig, stashed until
engine-stammer, whistle-shriek, the rolling vowels
of Wales, train hauling its song, station after station
like the faith we'd sworn we'd keep to fearful parents

who pressed addresses into our small town hands.
Cards marked, we played brag for the new money
we jingled in our fingers, trying to weigh its sovereign
otherness; and here comes England, a man in uniform

politely clipping tickets. His velvet midnight skin; the Irish
suddenly made sense of, Miss O'Kelly at the blackboard
drumming in the word for 'negro', *an fear gorm,* the blue man
who stands before us, asking if we know where we are going.

New Poems

Sunlight

What I remember thinking first when I walked in
as my sister turned and shook her head, saying "She's gone,"

is how the light continued pouring in through the big window
without pausing to acknowledge any sense

of what just happened, the sun's early brilliance landing
on the bedclothes, on the tubes and dials and switches,

and on the slumped flesh, the sunken cheekbones of my mother,
who seemed overnight to have been carved

out of marble by Bernini. And after we'd all embraced,
and I'd leaned in across the pillows to kiss her forehead

that was already cool against my lips, I thought
not of the years she'd carried me, and held me,

and then, when I'd insisted I was ready, let me go,
without ever really letting go, although I did think

later on, and later on again, about all these things, and more.
No, no: what I thought then was that this shameless,

brutal impulse to make art, no matter what; this itch,
when it comes crawling, that you can never scratch enough

meant that one day I would set down these tiny, useless marks
and somehow think that they were equal to all of this

or even to the sunlight falling for the last time
on my mother's face without occasion.

Café

after Edward Hopper's 'Automat'

Darkness gazes in this window
where you sit, a cup raised towards
freshly-crimsoned lips, waiting. Winter's
on the street; the café's warm, though you've
still got your coat on, and your hat, blue eyes
cast down beneath the cloche's brim, as if
these coffee grains could tell what's next for you,
or if what's broken ever might be mended.
Night presses its nose against the glass,
but this brightness within declares
a larger lonely; the ceiling-lamps speech bubbles,
saying nothing. Empty chairs. A brass rail,
leading nowhere. Your ungloved hand.
The radiator's mumbled Latin prayer.

Portrait of a Young Woman

A window facing north. Outside on the roadside
daffodils are sprouting under birches coming
tentatively into leaf, but in the studio the concrete floor
is bare. My mother shivers in her chair,
not knowing where to look and already wishing
she could leave. He's behind the easel,
the beard gone white but the eyes still glittering

as he scratches at the surface with the charcoal sticks
he clutches, marking out his territory
on paper: her eyes, her mouth, her hair.
Shading and filling in among the little mounds
of black dust he blows away or smudges.
My mother looks around: at the mirror
where he sometimes searches for an image

of himself; at the coat-stand draped with ghosts.
"This way," he growls, "this way, please."
He is eighty-one, more than twice her age,
the sickness that will kill him already blooming
in his gut as he wonders how many years his hands
have left. "Right," he says eventually,
"I'll let you know when it's ready." He does not

show it to her then, but three weeks later, when I
come home from school, the picture is sitting
on a chair, my mother and my father standing glumly
either side, like an out-take from the Nativity.
"What do you think?" my father asks me. I am ten
and know no image of my mother that is not perfect.
"It's nice," I say. My father frowns. My mother

looks away, uncomfortable at the attention and bemused
by the Aran woman she has become, dark-eyed,
hollow-cheeked, sallow-skinned. The picture
is sold quietly, and here the story ends, or almost does,
until forty-four years later, in the last year
of my mother's life, when the picture appears for auction,
listed as 'Portrait of a Young Woman'

by Sean Keating. The room is crowded; a flurry
of hands, and my mother is sold again, exceeding –
not for the first time – the expectations of others.
And this time the story does end, the way all our stories
end: bowed heads and cut flowers, a laid-out husk
we barely recognise, remade by others who etch in
their own loss, the way Keating remade his grief

in this image of a woman from the islands he so loved
but never again visited after his wife's death. Her eyes
wet capstones. Her mouth a wave at sea. Her hair
approaching rain; marks set down before
the moment passes that already are too late,
pure allegory in their making, and in what is made;
my mother, sitting still, becoming ash.

Nighthawks

I am polishing a pair of his black leather shoes
when he rings. It may as well be Long Distance
though he's not far, a few miles on this summer night
to where my father's calling from once more, to tell us
he'll be late. You hang up, and I can hear the absence
in your voice, weary as you turn to feign delight

admiring the great job I've done, the kitchen light
gleaming on the uppers of the empty shoes.
I'm twelve years old, but there is nothing new about this absence
as you explain again how hard he works, the distances
he must travel; how he would spend more time with us
but has to leave when the call comes, out into the night,

the doctor's bag beside him as he heads off, knight
in an old Jaguar, all business under ward light
as he arrives to tend to injured children just like us.
My little brother slept as anxious parents listened for his shoes
urgent on the corridor. They would cover any distance
to bring their children to him, afraid of the absence

this white-faced son or daughter might become. Never absent
when they needed him, he worked around the clock, as if night
was inseparable from day. At home I watched the distance
growing, growing. Sometimes you'd let me stay up late,
saucer-eyed in front of the TV while you gazed at your shoes,
sipped your drink and waited. Years after all of this, in the US

I saw those paintings by Hopper and thought of the two of us,
you and I: the sunlit rooms so lonely, filled with absence.
The empty highways at dusk. So many places where the heartache
    shows;

apartment-buildings, streets, the window on the corner in 'Night-
hawks', where a man and a woman are sitting up in diner-light;
there is another man across from them as well, but the distance

between them is far more than the counter, a distance
that seems to have been there for ever. At least like us
those two had each other, keeping each other company as the light
finally died. "But he still loves you. Always wanted to have sons
like you," you told me once, the bottle empty late one night
when a few more things got said. I showed my brother the shoes

then, resolved to keep my distance, afraid of what was happening
        to us
and what would happen after, in his absence. I switched out the
        light
and lay in bed at night, waiting to grow up. To fill my father's shoes.

The Breaststroke

In the azure swimming pool of the summer I turned twelve
my mother taught us how to do the breaststroke. Already
I knew everything, and quickly became bored while my sister,
younger and more patient always, listened carefully, and Helen

the third member of our little class, frowned anxiously, terrified
of water. She had come into our lives to tend to us when we
were small, and ended staying thirteen years, and now she stood
beside us in the shallow end, big-boned, russet-haired, milk-skinned,

not much more than a girl herself, her teeth chattering even though
the sun was high, the water warm. "First, stretch your hands out
shoulder-high in front of you. Then, turn your palms outwards
and spread your arms, as if opening a pair of curtains." Although not

a natural swimmer, my mother was an excellent teacher, diligent
to ensure that we would always know the right thing to do.
And would do it. "Now, pull your arms right down and push
the water backwards, past your hips." At the far end others

shrieked and and dive-bombed as we practised, my sister giggling,
and Helen wrinkling her nose up at the splashes. Neither of us then
knew anything of Helen's mother's story; how she'd been widowed
young and so, astray with grief, had chosen to walk into

the brown waters of the local river, leaving behind her seven daughters,
but the one thing my mother knew was that she was going to teach
this girl to swim. "Next, the kick." We held on to the edge and stretched
our legs behind us, as far as they would go. "Imagine you are a frog,"

my mother said, waving to my father, the dapper prince she'd kissed
who lay now on a sun-lounger, working his way through the paper:
Nastase, and Billie-Jean, and the Rebel County's prospects in the
    Final.
"You bring your feet together and crouch, like you were squatting

on a lily pad. Now, spring!" Our legs made diamonds; extend and
    thrust.
The water churned. "Now, arms and legs together, across the pool."
We lined up and pushed off; me powering ahead, keen to show
how quick I was, although my sister was already gaining ground

and Helen a distance behind both of us, trying to find a way between
our threshing limbs. She stopped. "I can't do this," she said.
"You can," replied my mother, "I know you can." My sister and I
watched from the far side as this girl slowly picked her own space

to swim into, parting carefully the waters until she touched
the edge beside us, smiling shyly, and all the time her head held high
above the surface, as if wearing a tiara. "You see!" my mother said,
whose generous heart always had found room for those

of little faith, "you see? Now, let's try going back". And we
went on, me and my sister, our widths becoming lengths, my
    sister
standing proudly on the podium at school meets, festooned
with dripping medals while I gave up the breaststroke, preferring

the headlong surge and flail of the front crawl, and Helen
moved on also, appearing only at weddings or at funerals,
still tall and pale, her red hair turned to grey, a twinkling man
now by her side, a man almost the same age as my father, a man

she married, and lived with quietly in a tall house by the coast.
Another of the things I know only now is that my mother always
    knew

the two of us could swim; that these lessons were not for me or
    for my sister,
but for Helen, an awkward, courteous girl who may sometimes

to my mother have seemed like an older daughter. And what
    better gift
can any mother give her daughter than to teach her how to stay
    afloat:
how to keep your head above water with grace, a grace my
    mother carried
with her her whole life, until she slipped away from us one
    summer morning,

not knowing – one of the few things she did not know – that a
    few weeks earlier
Helen had walked down the steps near where she lived into the
    sea,
and swum out as far as she could go until she could swim no
    longer,
and then bowed her head beneath the waves. And held it there.

Mackerel

i.m. Billo O'Donnell

Shouldering you through these streets
for the last time, how light you are in here,
battened down like any canny sailor
for the mother of a squall that's making its way over

the hill of headstones locals all agree
has the best views in town. Maybe I'm
just lucky I'm amidships, between heels
and head, the tall ones front and back taking

the weight of what's in there with you, bowlines
and anchor chain and South Sea frangipani,
or maybe this easy metaphor of pine
and brass we carry could no more hold you

than this box I'm making here, or any crate
unloaded from some greasy trawler stacked
with mackerel, arrowheads of silver dabbed
with darkness, each blank eye a black mirror

of what's gone. So slippery, this notion
of an after, one we love becoming other,
a shimmer, swerving into deeper water,
dart and flicker. And disappears, leaving us

these gleaming serried souls laid out on ice,
the solace of their iridescence, halo-scales
stuck to our fingers as we lower you over the side
of all we know, our eyes abrim with ocean

until the line tightens, begins to thrum
aboard the 'Colleen' fifty years astern,
you pointing at our wake and signaling to me
to start reeling in, my seven-year old

city-slicker hands shaking as I wind;
and every hook is taken, the whole line wriggling
with life, and you laughing like there's no tomorrow,
foam and spray rainbowing the air.

Wreckfish

for Hughie O'Donoghue

Rust-mottled from a lifetime spent
in weed and sand, indigo gloom,
the seabed's slither-suck

while other shoals go busily
about their business, and what
I'm looking for I still don't know

but I'll keep looking anyway,
grey-jowled, battle-scarred,
going deeper for what's hidden

in among these rotten timbers
other lives stowed in the hold,
secrets gone down with the ship,

old hurts, lies and silences,
though there are nights when I can hear
the heave and haul of oar-music

above me, each splash breaking
the skin; glimpse of strakes and rivets,
a sky barnacled with stars,

and sometimes then a song of longing
rises shyly to the surface,
stashed cargo the ones below

had also taken with them, a tune
astounded boatmen will later swear
came out of nowhere, and was always there.

The Tide

This morning, a new offering
on the altar of the strand: a young
bull seal, left behind after last night's
acts of war, his wounds carnelian,
still fresh. The others watch him
from the water, their gleaming,
whiskery heads diving and then
popping up, standing off or swerving
close to witness his once-sleek flesh
becoming rock. One of their own.

But when he dies they disappear, leaving
what is left of him alone; no dreams of sunlit
oceans, herring-throngs, since we dream these for him
instead. We put on black, and stand for songs
and weep because we cannot let go, ever,
of our dead, or bear to think that this is all there is,
this foam-frilled beach which tomorrow will be
empty; and the sea, that we can just about
make out from the window of this corridor
where we are gathered, waiting for the tide.

The Bad Thief

We'd had to wait while someone went for nails.
The soldiers stood around us, eating dates.
I'd seen him once before, and heard the stories,
though how on earth he'd ended up like this,
with the two of us for company, I don't know.
A wind that smelt of hyssop-leaves. When I offered him
my hand one big bruiser clanked his sword.
"Word is," I whispered, "you could save us all.
Well, now's your chance!" Admit it: you'd have done
the same. But he just sighed: "Too late for me,
though not for you." His pale hand small in mine
as they came towards us with the hammer. *One
redeemed, and one condemned*, some hack scribbled later.
But what was there between us in the end?

The Convertible

Evenings they'd cruise these streets in moult,
windows wound down, each radio thumping out
its carnal beat, high-fives on reds before the fuel-injected
jolt, the foot-down, flat-out roar of engines

and the whoops of crew-necked gods. They'd wave
and toot their horns at him as he stood watching
from the high windows of this house I'd paid for
by a life-time at El Sol, the factory my own father'd built

that I still drove to every day, dawn till dusk, in the fin-tailed
gold convertible gleaming in our driveway. She was
heaven-sent, one of a kind, a Phaethon Deluxe V8
automatic, her white tyres shining steeds hoofing

the ground. He shone too, this son of mine, and he was
mine, no matter what some folk said about my ex,
and when he turned his blond curls towards me I looked away,
afraid of what was coming. "If you really loved me

you would let me." Anything but this, I begged him,
knowing she'd be too much for him. Knowing that he'd never
rein her in. But he'd his heart set; how could I refuse?
His grin as she erupted at the slightest touch of pedal;

when he eased her out the gate he waved back once
before he gave her holly, scorching off into the distance,
heading west. Ahead the highway, the hot tar's
shimmering meniscus, and the quivering, open mouth

of the earnest young policeman
later on the doorstep, his hands twisting the cap

he's respectfully removed, the night behind lit up
by the squad car's pulsing blues. "Bad bend,"

he said, his words becoming torn metal, the pylon
buckling on impact, jags of lightning hissing
from the writhing cables, and the river churning
where they'd found his catapulted body

in the ravine far below. O my beautiful, my broken son!
Now he rises once again, borne skywards by the helicopter's
dripping slings, over the stricken poplars and the silent chorus
gathered on the roadside, as if this machine hovering above us

could reel in all of this, could unwind time to a time
before the dying fall of light: the sun-struck streets,
still empty, waiting for the songs of cars. A boy
dreaming of oil and chrome. As if we could go back.

Mummers

A tinseled bucket shaken by tipsy singers
belting out the old ones in the mall
is the wassail-cup those other players carried

town to town, through frost and rime,
their tasseled revels and bright songs
ribboning the winter thorn. Their promise

of our heart's desire if we'll but pay their tune.
I handsel bronze, and somehow hear
among these red-cheeked voices

her wavery contralto, proclaiming
what she called her blindfold faith
in a hereafter I too want to believe in,

that I might see her once again,
and open my own mouth to sing,
but grief's an anvil on my tongue.

Their ancient dumbshow: death,
and then rebirth; a potion's magic charms.
The actors bow, and disappear,

become a silence named in stone.
My mother underneath Glasnevin clay
asleep in her own mother's bony arms.

The Thaw

So solid at first you'd stake your life on it –
morning dazzle, world made pure and raw.
Shouts of lovers trading snowballs

on streets that will be silent, slump
of slush mid-afternoon, roofs
already weeping at the thaw.

The Lucas Planet No. 33

i.m. Seamus Heaney

I
Say first a sup of kerosene, poured deftly into the squat casing
at the base, and then a match scratched into action, held flare-
    headed,
steady-handed in the opened porthole, your other hand turning
the handle so that the wick rose like a cobra charmed to greet
the flame, the enamelled blackness of the chamber suddenly aglow
in its own solstice. The cover then snapped shut, the spring-hinge
bracket-clipped beneath the handlebars and you're off,
a leg swung easy over the saddle, your wavering front beam
diminishing the evening lengthening between us until you
    disappear.

II
Then say another oil, a different kind of light:
sweet balm of chrism and the spear-tipped flames of candles,
white flowers hushing the room, and you in your good suit,
as ready as you can be for the journey, the ditches lined
with curious schoolchildren and stout policemen saluting as you
    pass
on your way north to where we lay you down between sycamore
    and ash,
low prayers and beak-twitter and murmured choked goodbyes,
and afterwards the hydraulic stutter of the digger,
its swung bucket a hero's empty helmet, scooping up and filling in
the opened ground; a lifetime's earth.

III

But now the way ahead is unlit, unapproved; no knowing
what may come hurtling without warning from the hedgerows,
oblivion in wait behind each trembling leaf, and nothing equal
to the darkness of this grief except perhaps the Lucas Planet
    No. 33,
the long-gone manufacturer's proud boast emblazoned on the
    box it comes in:
"*We make light of our labours,*" and for a moment the world is
    once more lit
by the power-surge of your grin, delighting in the pun, and
    crediting as well
the credo of all art: to make the effort made seem effortless while
    going
to the heart of what matters. Actual and emblem, this venerable
    bicycle-lamp;
sturdy, trustworthy, the heft of it a kind of grace, and this time I
    take off,
unsteadily; still sad, and fearful, yes: uncertain where I'm going
but gladdened by this ghost-light, the road before me
    brightening
in its occult and familiar gleam. Wheel-spin; spoke-song.
The consolation that what's well-made endures, and shines on.

If You Have To Ask, You'll Never Know

A flutter through the pockets
of the dead Confederate's jacket,
his fingers searching for shiny things

but the boy's already been picked clean;
belt-buckle, buttons gone, and he's moving
to the next slumped uniform when he sees it,

half-sunk in a mud-rut left behind by the artillery,
crimson splotches on intestines of coiled brass
the bell-mouth a burnished O, and so he lifts it

to his lips, tasting the grits and bitter coffee,
the dead kid's final meal. The noise he makes first try
is like the squawking of an irritable hen

but the second time, when he blows,
is different, rising over field-holler, cotton-songs,
high as moon, a midnight picture hung above

the Mississippi, paddle-steamer's steady churning,
and here's another one, aboard the Sunny South
among the card-sharks and the carpet-baggers,

florid gentlemen and fine young ladies, and waiters
and kitchen-mizzies, and cabin-boys just like him, though no one
plays like he does, the notes he plays, and doesn't play,

the air in the saloon swollen with heat; the men
nodding along, tap-tapping their shoes and eyeing up
the women, who are also watching, rapt, wondering

what this sound is called, and what other buttons
these dark hands might press. He fingers valves,
eases in and out the slide, and on the river rolls

to New Orleans, the working girls of Storyville
fixing their hair while this one plays, his cheeks
swollen like a satchel filled with pennies

on the corner; and here he is out on the road
that took so many of them, the truck loaded
with reel-to-reels and jelly-rolls, red beans

and ricely yours, white folk staring as they pass,
and sometimes their own hissing 'Uncle Tom,' while they
keep squeezing out those cantaloupes of sound,

so juicy and so sweet, arpeggios and trills bent
into the shape of sex and hunger and desire,
alongside the others: a monk bent in prayer

over the keys, another dusting artfully the skins and cymbals,
keeping the swing, and now one raises up the great gold carp
of his saxophone, train-noise piercing the blue night,

and one standing behind them in a pork-pie hat,
plucking at a stringed wardrobe for its syncopated heart,
but if the saints by some chance ever do

go marching in I want to be up there
with the horns, Miles and Dizzy, Freddie Hubbard,
and Satchmo, and all the other cats

who'll know a little place, no questions asked,
with good tunes and decent liquor where we can all go
after the encore's last note has sounded.

Postcard

Imagine one arriving out of nowhere,
out of the blue of this place at high tide;
this fishing-net, say, washed up on the shore
that now becomes the veil worn by a bride:
merrow-flowers, union of knots and splices,
torn strands where something bigger's gotten through
to where you sit: this desk, this room. It pauses,
looks you in the eye, moves on, and nothing you
make here can ever hold it; these tangled lines
the best that you can do. No matter. Send this
anyway; post it off, hoping it finds
its scribbled destination; the address
already fading, the words for all this gone,
and no knowing where the next is coming from.

Veteran

The young whore's eyes so carefully averted
are the blue the Irish nurse was wearing

when she took his pulse and gazed at the blank space
at the far end of the ward, where a mirror

had by order been removed. He moves on
through the night, these streets he'd fought for,

a world he'd helped to save now shrunken
to a bare-bulb bedsit room, meat teas alone,

the distant roar of terraced Saturdays and evenings
in The Palace, the off-white taped-up screen

billowing in the darkness. Ratscrabble
under footlights. And all around the unconscripted

laughter, jeers; the urgent, unarmed combat
between pasty-faced young men and whippet girls

who flinch at what Herr Sniper's left behind
to haunt this seaside town, which trembled

when the guns had boomed in France, the flags
out on the links rattling in their cups,

but does not now appear especially grateful,
in spite of the memorial dutifully erected

in the square. Where once a boy
had pointed at the pulped eye-socket, stew

of cartilage and bone, the crater where
a nose and cheek had been, whispering

"That man's got no face," his voice
a small clear bell ringing *unclean.*

Pterygium *

Perhaps the genus of that cloud
slicing an Andalusian moon
to the *a capella* barking of a dog

that isn't there. Or the Latin for
that bird, flickering just once
across the Empire State Building

in the grainy black and white
of Warhol's eight-hour stare.
Here is your own home movie: blink

and you miss it. I lean back
in the chair, wondering if
I've heard her right, and how much

I've got left as she asks me
to read Snellen, man of letters,
off the wall. I squint

at the chart. So little at the end,
after so much: this is what's ahead,
and what's behind. She presses

a phial of tears into my hand.
"Take these," she says, "and see me
in a year." And if she is a sorceress

straight out of Grimm, I am
joker in the land of the half-blind,
plucking nervously these strings, aware

of something happening in the corner
of my eye, motley fading as I sing
against the dark that's outside, gathering.

* A growth of tissue on the conjunctiva of the eye

151

Swim

Don't loiter in the shallows. Just wade in:
slowly if you want at first, but not too slow.
Embrace the chill of it, brimming up around you;
feel it seep into your skin. Keep going further,
deeper, even though you've no idea of what's
down there, or what you might come up with.
Stretch yourself. Inhale the amniotic stink; become
weightless, a raft of sinew, limb. Soon you'll be
out of sight of everything you've left behind,
buoyant and adrift amid its scales and echoes.
Don't panic. All that you can see is all that matters.
So don't look back. And don't give in. Take this breath
as if it were your last, and then the next
the same. Put your head down. Now, swim.